Nelson –

I was so glad to walk out in the freezing cold dark night of Lima to get this book for you from my trunk. But you are worth it buddy!

Mike

10/25/18

don't forget ~~~ www. michaelschoenhofer.com

Stumbling Into Happiness

A Catholic Priest Finds True Love in Wild Places

MICHAEL SCHOENHOFER

© Michael Schoenhofer 2017

Print ISBN: 978-1-54391-003-2

eBook ISBN: 978-1-54391-004-9

Acknowledgements

I owe a huge debt of gratitude to my editor, Ann Kaiser, who spent months meticulously going over every sentence of the first two drafts and taught me how to find my inner writer. I appreciate so much her enthusiasm for this project. Thanks to my wife, Mary, who read the entire manuscript out loud with me and laughed appropriately at funny moments in our story. My three children, Stephanie, Kara, and Mark, inspired me to write this memoir. They have been telling "the story" since sixth grade while I lived in ignorant bliss that my past was still unknown. Guys, here's what ACTUALLY happened.

Dedication

For Mary, Stephanie, Kara, and Mark

Introduction

The plane was taking me to Perth, a nine-hour flight from Harare, the capital of Zimbabwe. A few days ago I was living in the bush and in a few hours I'd be landing in Australia. What a change! The last few years were full of changes, experiences, and drama. Laying in the sand with two AK 47 assault rifles pointed at my head, chasing a rhino down a dirt road, hanging upside down from seat belts in the middle of nowhere. It all seemed so unlikely for a regular guy from Toledo, Ohio.

What was I getting myself into now? I'd said "yes" to studying in Rome in 1973 and that was an adventure. I'd said "yes" to coming to Africa in 1983 and even more adventure. Now here it was Christmas time in 1988 and I'd said "yes" to going to Australia.

Let's rewind this story to the summer of 1983 with this simple question - "Mike, how would you like to go to Africa?"

Chapter 1

Toledo October 1983

I will never forget that summer day in 1983 when Hoffman asked me to go to Africa. That was the year I turned 31. I lived at the Cathedral in Toledo with him - Hoffman was the Bishop. He planned to send a team of three to the Diocese of Hwange in Zimbabwe. The bishop already chose two sisters, and he needed a priest to join the team. I had been a priest for almost six years. I didn't like being a priest. Periodically during my years in college and graduate school, I would tell a counselor, "I'm quitting," which meant I didn't want to study for the priesthood anymore. My announcement usually came after I had fallen in love with a girl. But I always found myself getting talked into staying a little while longer. "Let the passion wear off a bit," the counselor advised. But then I'd meet another girl and fall in love all over again. In April 1972 I went on a study trip to Kentucky over Easter break during my junior year in college. By the end of that week, I had fallen in love again. She had long red hair, pale skin, and freckles all over her face. I dated her all through the next summer in Toledo. She lived at Mercy Hospital studying to be a nurse while I was across town at St. Teresa Parish doing an internship. Dating never made the "recommended activity list" for an aspiring priest. I talked to the priest living in the parish,

Fr. Bernie, about the fact that I was falling in love. "Give it another year," he advised. At the end of the summer I broke it off with her, and it broke my heart. The Bishop sent me to Rome, Italy to get the required degree in theology to become an ordained priest. I shipped out to Rome in August of 1973, sailing out of New York on the Italian Lines ship, the Raffaello. I also kissed goodbye to any hope of getting back to my girlfriend again. My love life suffered, but my travel life was beginning to flourish.

Four years later, I was ordained a priest and assigned to St. Mary's Church in Tiffin, Ohio, which just happened to be the hometown of the red haired girl I left four years earlier! The street where her parents lived in Tiffin also bore her last name, a painful reminder to me of what I had given up. I frequently had to drive by that awful street on my way to the hospital or to visit a parishioner. Seeing her name on that street sign was so upsetting that as I drove near the street, I would close my eyes so I wouldn't have to see her name. It made the moment a bit perilous for other drivers. On one occasion I failed to yield to another driver who was pulling through the intersection. I slammed on the brakes just in time to see her give me "the bird." Our eyes met. She saw my Roman Collar and pulled over to the side of the street, got out of the car, and began to apologize. I recognized her as a member of my parish.

In June of 1980, I received a letter reassigning me from St. Mary's in Tiffin to the Cathedral in Toledo. The Bishop transferred young priests to a different parish every three years. I enjoyed the people in Tiffin but was glad to be putting some space between me and that street. Toledo was my hometown, and it felt good to be closer to old friends and family. Early on Tuesday, July 1, I took off in my little yellow VW Bug which was packed to the roof with all my stuff and headed north. My friend Fr. Bernie and I spent what should have been my first full day at the Cathedral, fishing.

Bernie had just purchased a new boat, and he wanted to take me out on it. "We'll go out for a few hours. The perch are biting. As long as you get to your new assignment before sunset," he said, "you'll be fine."

"But I get seasick," I said.

"The lake is calm. You'll be fine."

Early that evening, after losing everything I ate into Lake Erie, and well before sunset, I arrived at the Cathedral parish.

"I thought you'd be here a lot earlier," the pastor said.

Apparently, the pastor had never heard of the sunset clause Bernie told me about earlier. I didn't tell him that I'd been fishing with Bernie. He showed me to my room and left me to unpack. The next three years I said Mass, visited parishioners and taught sophomores at Central Catholic High School three days a week. I became the last resort for students who found themselves "on the ropes." My classes at Central Catholic kept growing throughout the year and soon over 40 students packed into my little classroom. It wasn't unusual for a new student to show up at my classroom door. On one occasion a tall young man with long hair stood to wait for me to let him into the room. I recognized him as one of the junior varsity football players.

"Can I help you?" I asked.

"Yah. They told me that if I couldn't make it in your class, they'd kick me out of school," he said.

"Come on in."

During that time Bernie and I started a soup kitchen on Dorr Street in Toledo and named it Claver House, after the first black saint, St. Peter Claver. The soup kitchen was in an old store front right next to the parish. All of the other soup kitchens closed on Sunday, so that is the day we decided to serve. Each week a different church would adopt the soup kitchen and bring in casseroles. The two of us would often approach the Bishop about expanding the work of this little effort by living together in a small house in Toledo and doing work with the poor. Nothing ever came of our requests. On the one hand, I wanted to live with Bernie in a simple house in the inner city, but I was living with the Bishop in his mansion.

The Bishop's house looked like a replica of the White House in the middle of Toledo; a huge, three-story home with four large, white, fluted pillars that stood two stories high over a grand entrance. The mansion included a ballroom on the third floor which the Bishop had converted into a chapel. There was even a solarium on the ground floor. I liked the idea of living with the poor, but I enjoyed the luxury of my rooms in a mansion. During those three years, I made good friends with a few nuns in Toledo and some other women with whom I'd go to dinner or the movies or a concert. If I couldn't get married, at least I could enjoy female companionship. Now I didn't feel lonely all the time. Sometimes with Bernie, my women friends, and my students, I felt momentary relief from an ever-present, lurking loneliness.

When the Bishop asked me to leave the life I had cobbled together in Toledo to go to Africa, I told him, "I'll think about it. But don't hold your breath." I thought, "I'll just humor him until this all goes away." But the lark turned into something different. In the two months since he'd asked me to go to Africa, I'd gotten caught up in some wild metaphysical and spiritual roller coaster. Passages from the Bible reached out and grabbed me. My prayer life became almost mystical. Even the radio and television seemed to have messages for me. I couldn't read anything without something in it touching my soul. I started to talk all "religious and spiritual," which scared all of my friends, who knew me as more of a jaded cynic.

At one point, a close friend asked, "What is happening to you?"

"I am in love with Jesus," I said. That answer disturbed us both.

Two months later, I stood in front of a discernment committee with two other priests who were also thinking about going to Africa. The Bishop gave them the power to pick one of us to be the third member of the team. The committee met with the three priests every week. At each meeting, we reported our thoughts and feelings about going to Africa. In October, after two months of these meetings and the constant spiritual battering I was experiencing, I felt confident and relieved for the first time. I had received a clear message from some other-worldly being in which I understood that I would not be going to Africa after all. The end to this whole charade was near. I heard an inner voice say, "Stop worrying about what comes next. Let go and trust in higher forces. Everything will work out." I couldn't wait until the committee met. Now I could get back to my "normal life" again. A week later I pulled up in front of a red brick ranch which was the home of the two Franciscan sisters who had already been chosen for the mission team. This is where the committee met with us every few weeks. I parked my new red Ford Escort under a glowing street light near the house and felt my stomach tense as I walked up to the front door in the early autumn chill and rang the bell. One of the priests opened the door. I could see everyone already seated and waiting for me.

"We are ready to start," he said. He took my coat and ushered me into the living room. The three priests of the discernment committee dressed in black shirts, black pants, and white clerical collars sat behind a long table. All three of the candidates sat on chairs facing them. This time I also noticed that the two sisters joined us. The atmosphere felt a little like I was in a courtroom. We began with a prayer asking the Holy Spirit to help us. Then the priest in charge asked each of us to talk about anything we had experienced in the past week, the same question he asked every week. He was trying to find out if any of us had received a message from the higher beings. I couldn't wait for my turn to speak. The other two candidates did not have much to say. I felt more and more anxious about the message I heard. That exuberant confidence left me and in its place crept in the sense of foreboding.

The chairman of the committee turned to me, "Mike, how has the past week been for you?"

I hesitated then said, "I have come to the point in this process where I don't care what you people do. I could stay here. I could go to Africa. I could go to Timbuktu. This discernment process is over for me. I don't give a shit about any of this anymore."

There was a long pause after my statement. The faces of the committee members looked both surprised and puzzled. There were some whispered exchanges between the chair of the committee and the others. "Please step into the kitchen for a few moments," the chairman told us, "we need time alone to discuss what has just happened."

With that, the three of us priests and the two women walked down the hall and into the kitchen, and the door closed behind us.

I felt the old Mike return. I loved the phrases "you people" and "don't give a shit." I had driven the nail into the "Africa" coffin, at last, I thought. From the kitchen, we could hear a murmur of discussion in the other room. One of my fellow candidates looked at me, "That was quite a speech."

I didn't know what to say.

A few minutes later the door opened, and the chairman of the committee said, "We'd like you all to reassemble in the living room now."

We followed him down the hallway and into the living room where we took our seats. Now I felt like the accused facing the jury. The three of us sat facing the three priests behind the long table. There was silence.

Then the chairman of the committee looked at us all and then straight to me, "Michael Schoenhofer has been chosen by the Holy Spirit and by us to be the priest on the mission team to Zimbabwe."

The "I am in love with Jesus" thing had gone way too far. The Metaphysical Presence had tricked me. I believed that if I just trusted more everything would work out fine. This was not fine! Sister Marge, whom the Bishop appointed to lead the team, was incredulous. Tears streaked down her face. The other priest, also named Mike coincidentally, had wanted to go to Africa. Maybe this Metaphysical Presence had gotten confused between the two Mike's. The other Mike had cooked up this whole "let's all go to the missions" thing together with Marge. What went wrong? I was speechless. The other two priests congratulated me, and I could see the relieved look on their faces. After about 20 minutes we all left. I don't remember much about the drive back to the Cathedral that night. I was in shock.

Over the next few months, I announced to my family, the Cathedral, and my friends about the decision of the committee to assign me to Africa. The three team members (the two sisters and me) all applied for our travel visas and work permits immediately. We didn't know how long it would take for our visas to be approved. I didn't know if I'd still be home at Thanksgiving or Christmas. Month after month we waited. Over time the reaction from my friends and parishioners did not diminish. After Sunday Mass, a long line of people waited to talk to me, to shake my hand and look into my eyes, as if to say, "Are you sure you want to do this?" But what could I do now?

The other team members, Marge and Julitta, had received months of mission team preparation at Maryknoll in New York. Marge had visited Zimbabwe already with the other Fr. Mike. Everything happened so quickly that I hadn't had any time to prepare to be a missionary. I asked them if I should go somewhere to get some training too. But these two women, who had already waited for months to go to Africa, didn't want to sit around any longer waiting for me to get trained.

"We'll take care of training you," Marge told me.

With no preparation, I was going to go live in another hemisphere, speak another language, and learn a new culture. I should have felt excited about this new adventure. But I felt helpless and alone. I sat and waited and wailed along with my family, my friends, and my parish, unsure of what these higher forces had in store for me next.

(Photo: Marge, Hoffman, Julitta at Victoria Falls)

Chapter 2

Toledo, Ohio to Hwange,

Zimbabwe February 1984

———— ◄ ► ————

I t was six months from the time Hoffman first asked me about going to Africa until the moment I got onto a plane. The three of us chosen to be on this first team from Toledo all came with different experiences. Marge had lived in Brazil as a missionary for five years. She was quite a bit shorter than my 6' 3" frame and wore her salt-and-pepper hair short. The other sister, Julitta, had worked in parishes all her life. She had a softer frame and brown hair and she liked a dab of lip gloss. I had lived in Europe for four years and by that time had become fluent in Italian and pretty good in German. Marge had the missionary experience, Julitta had pastoral experience, and I had language experience and could say Mass. But other than that, we had no idea how to start a mission from scratch. The visas for Marge and I came through first.

Marge decided that we shouldn't wait for Julitta. "We don't know how long it's going to take for Julitta to get her visa. I want to get started," she said. "We can meet up with her in Zimbabwe. That will give us some time to get things going."

"OK boss," I thought. The thermometer hit the 40's on that Friday afternoon, February 10, 1984, when I drove with Mom and Dad to the airport in Detroit. We arrived way too early and waited around forever to board the evening flight to London. My brother Don and his wife Joan and my nephew Justin, along with my sister Janet and her husband John, and my brother Fred also made the trip to the airport to see me off. The anxiety and feeling of sadness at my leaving them for three years heightened the longer we stood around waiting. We had all anticipated this moment for months. Marge and I boarded the plane around 7:00 PM for the long flight to London. We arrived at Heathrow the next morning and then boarded a connecting flight around noon for Madrid, Spain arriving there in mid-afternoon. Marge had arranged for us to meet with the Spanish priests now living in Madrid who had worked in Zimbabwe before. We both hoped these experienced missionaries would give us some insight into mission life in Zimbabwe where we were going to work. Madrid at that time of the year hit the high 50's and at night sank into the 20's. It rained every day while we were there.

The priests "central command" was in a suburb of Madrid, just a short subway ride from the airport. It looked like an apartment house in the middle of a residential neighborhood. A tiny sign near the door identified it as the "Instituto Español de San Francisco Javier para Misiones Extranjeras." We just called them the Spanish Priests. Marge and I each had a tiny room with a bed, a table, and a chair. We walked down the hall to a bathroom and shower area. It wasn't five star, but the price was right - free! There was just one tiny problem - no heating. Add to that the damp air, and I froze even under heaps of blankets. We didn't learn much more from them than we already knew. But we did enjoy a few bottles of Spanish table wine the priests opened with a bottle opener, and we got to see Madrid, Toledo, and parts of the surrounding countryside. I was disappointed that I never got the orientation to Zimbabwe and to mission life I had expected. The priests were more interested in entertaining us and showing us the sights. After five days we flew to Munich to visit my German cousins whom I'd gotten to know well as a student while studying in Rome. They lived in a beautiful five-floor condominium in the Swabbing District of Munich. Each day Marge and I would trek out into the city to see the sites. One day we ventured into the Hofbrau Haus and drank beer, ate pretzels and brats, and chatted with the locals. My cousin Robert gave us some good advice over some great German beer. He told us to make sure the people felt like they were getting some economic benefit from us.

"Don't be too religious," he said in a thick German accent, "they have to feel better off financially."

We didn't believe him. Our motives were purer than that. But his advice would ring truer than we thought.

Marge had traveled to Zimbabwe a year earlier with the other Mike to scope out our mission. Marge's no nonsense demeanor earned her the nickname "Sarge" from some of my fellow priests. Ten days, three continents, and two hemispheres later, we landed in Harare, Zimbabwe's capital. The stewardess opened the door and even at 7:00 in the morning the tropical air rushed into the plane like a thick syrup. The ground crew rolled a stairway up to the opened hatch, and we all lined up to deplane. I picked my way down the stairs trying to pay attention to each step while looking around at this new world. A slight breeze rustled the branches of the palm trees that grew everywhere. They made a cracking sound like a spoon on a wooden bowl followed by the swoosh of the long palm fronds. The tarmac steamed in the early morning heat. I walked into the terminal where rows of chairs lined the lounge. Marge and I found a pair of empty seats and sat down to regroup. These chairs looked like they'd come from an old Greyhound bus terminal, the legs, and backs made of tubular chrome and the seats covered in cracked red vinyl. A few spinning fans moved the stifling air in the small transit lounge. I expected to see Indiana Jones appear at any moment. Marge figured out that our next flight to Victoria Falls wouldn't leave for three more hours, so we waited and sweated until boarding time. It never occurred to me that Zimbabwe was in the tropics.

The people at the Cathedral had given me a big safari helmet at a going away party they held for me in the gymnasium, but I thought it was just a joke. I wished I had it now.

We boarded a small prop jet and took off for Victoria Falls around 10:00 that the morning. Now I could see the landscape as we flew over the country and it looked like a desert to me - a hot desert. We flew low enough so that I caught glimpses of traditional villages where people lived in round houses with grass thatch roofs. We flew over small towns and vast areas that looked pretty desolate. The flight took two hours. I felt airsick as the plane bumped along at a lower altitude. Where the airport in Harare steamed, the airport in Victoria Falls sizzled. Two Spanish Priests of the same order we visited in Madrid met us in the small terminal. They took us to the Victoria Falls Hotel for a Coke. With the first sip of this magic elixir, I felt better. Sitting in the hotel garden, surrounded by palm trees and flowering plants, everything looked exotic and otherworldly, like something out of an old movie. Fr. Joseph, our driver, told us that the hotel had 180 guest rooms and a grand dining room. A short walk from where we sat was one of the Natural Wonders of the World: Victoria Falls.

"We don't have time to show you the Falls today," he said, "we'll save that for later."

I didn't have a lot more tourist in me at that point after Madrid and Munich. I could see myself coming here for refreshment after months in the bush. I couldn't wait to write home about this.

Then Father Joseph said, "Let's go to Hwange," like someone would say, "Let's go to Disneyland," and we were off.

Marge and I rode in the back of Fr. Joseph's small white Renault. It rattled along the highway showing off its age. I told Fr. Joseph that this road seemed nicer than I had anticipated. I expected something a little more rugged, sandy, and "bush-like."

"This is the super highway from Hwange to Bulawayo," he said, "pull off to the right or the left, and within a few yards the roads are rutted dirt and sand. Do you want to try one?"

"No thanks," Marge and I said.

We wanted to land someplace for a few days and stop moving. We drove by the villages we had just flown over on our flight from Harare.

Fr. Joseph told us, "the small homes are called rondavels."

Each house was round with a painted mud exterior and a grass thatch roof. We saw exotic trees along the road different from all the palms we'd seen in Harare and Victoria Falls. The oddest one, Fr. Joseph told us, was the Baobab tree. The trunk of the tree was at least 30 feet around, and its branches looked like roots sticking up in the air as if someone had planted it upside down. We saw women carrying baskets on their heads or grinding corn into meal using large mortars and pestles. After an hour we arrived in Hwange. A wide grassy median planted with palm trees and more of those unknown flowering bushes grew in the middle of a wide boulevard. The shops on one side of the street looked like something out of the old west; one-story structures with awnings that covered the sidewalk. We stopped at the Franciscan convent where Marge would stay. The English and Irish sisters who ran the hospital invited us in for a cup of tea and some biscuits. Then the priests took Marge and me to the Bishop's House. We arrived in time for lunch, just before siesta.

Bishop Prieto tumbled out of the house, eager to greet us.

"Welcome Michael. Welcome, Marge. So glad to finally meet you."

The bishop was short and stout with a permanent smile and laugh lines around his eyes. He sparkled. I liked him. We ate chicken and rice followed by a fruit basket. I chose a big red apple from the basket. The Bishop reached out and grabbed my arm as I raised the apple to my mouth.

"No Michael, you must peel it first. The skin is full of poisons from the spraying."

The apple looked pretty sad after I finished peeling it. There was more flesh left on the skin than got into my mouth. Marge looked disgusted.

Fr. Joseph drove Marge back to the convent, and the Bishop showed me to my room for a siesta. The midday heat was stifling. The Bishop's House was a one-story, rambling structure, built of cement block. My room was small with a twin bed, a desk and chair, a standing closet to hang clothes, and a sink. It had a small window up near the ceiling with the curtains drawn. I checked for pythons and scorpions under my bed before I unpacked my luggage. Then I found myself standing in the middle of the room staring at the bed. I'd anticipated this moment of arrival for so long. But rather than feeling the excitement, I felt grief and loss and an intense loneliness. I shook my head and cried. What was happening to me? It reminded me of the same grief I felt the day after my ordination six and a half years earlier. I stood in my parents' basement as I waited to report to my first assignment the next day asking just about the same question, "What had I gotten myself into?"

Marge and I hung out in Hwange for a few days, getting over jet lag and acclimating to the tropical climate. Then we set off by bus back to Harare via Bulawayo to get the last piece of paperwork we needed - our resident's visas. The ten-day trip across Europe as well as the wine and beer we shared had broken the ice between us. Marge possessed a sharp tongue and a determined manner, but I saw a fun-loving side to her, and I admired her love of adventure.

The luxury coach we rode to Bulawayo had upholstered seats that reclined but no air conditioning. The windows opened to let in a hot breeze. Boarding the bus to Bulawayo, we felt excited about being on our own in Africa. As we made our way south through forests and savannas, I saw the occasional giraffe, warthog, and impala on the side of the road. After four hours, the coach passed more houses made of brick with peaked shingled roofs instead of the rondavels we had seen earlier. We drove through the suburbs, where the houses became more numerous along wide side streets. The hustle and bustle of the city stunned me. Marge stayed with the Franciscan Sisters who ran another hospital in Bulawayo while I went to a parish run by the Spanish priests. We explored the city for a few days and discovered department stores, movie theaters, and restaurants. Then we boarded another coach to Harare. Bulawayo looked like a place where I could enjoy a nice meal and a movie occasionally.

On the drive from Bulawayo, we saw many more farms and small towns along the grassy plains of Zimbabwe. The walls of the homes were well-maintained, and they were all decorated with brightly painted zig-zagging lines. The thatch on the roof was thick, and the people were better dressed. The women wore brightly colored wraps, and the men wore western style pants and shirts. We saw trucks, tractors, and other vehicles in each village. It looked much more affluent than the villages we had seen around Hwange.

While I struggled with all of the change in climate and environment, Marge loved it.

"I can't believe we are in Africa. Isn't this great?" Then she began to list everything we needed, everything she wanted to see, and people she wanted to meet. She saw each challenge as an adventure, no matter how much time it took. She also enjoyed relaxing in the evenings with an adult beverage. "Let's get out of here," she told me once we arrived at the convent in Harare, "and see if we can find a beer somewhere."

We arrived in Zimbabwe four years after the end of a long civil war. Tensions still boiled between the ruling Shona Tribe ZANU and the Ndebele Tribe ZAPU. Some areas of the country still experienced the remnants of war. ZAPU guerrilla fighters controlled the area around Bulawayo. Marge didn't mind. She had lived on the streets doing mission work with the poor for some years. She was aware of the danger but didn't shrink from it.

We stayed with the German Dominican Sisters in Harare. They welcomed us with sausage and sauerkraut, just like the English and Irish sisters had welcomed us with tea and biscuits and the Spanish priests with chicken and rice. The international community lived in the culture but managed to retain bits of their own, especially when it came to food. Marge and I were different. We were Americans. Most people only saw Americans in the movies. While the Franciscan Sisters in Hwange and Bulawayo ran hospitals, these Dominican nuns ran schools. A large elementary and high school stood right in the middle of the convent compound. The noise of the traffic and the people on the streets of the city ceased when we walked through the convent gates into an eerie quiet, removed from the outside world.

The convent took up an entire city block, surrounded by high walls topped with shards of broken glass. It looked like a medieval battlement meant to deter thieves from sneaking into the convent grounds and had provided the sisters and their students a sense of safety during the civil war. Courtyards and gardens hid among the gleaming white buildings on the convent grounds. Marble lined the interior of the large convent chapel, as big as any parish church at home. Many sisters taught in the school in Harare or their mission schools out in the countryside. The rest of the sisters took care of the large convent plant; laundry, cooking, gardening, financial, etc. I found myself getting lost in the maze of hallways, court-yards, and buildings. Some German sister would often find me wandering and gently escort me out of a restricted area.

A few days after we arrived, Marge realized she had forgotten her pass-port in Hwange.

"You stay here," she told me, "I want to make this trip on my own. Now you will have a chance to do some exploring."

She went back by a coach while I remained at the Dominican convent. The wait for her return took longer than I expected. And some unexpected things happened that would provide me with the orientation to life in Africa I was seeking. Higher forces seemed to be at work.

Chapter 3

Harare February 1984

―――――――

While I waited for Marge to return, I celebrated Mass for the Dominican Sisters every day and wandered around the city. It was the middle of the summer in the Southern Hemisphere, so I kept my wandering to the morning. The sisters told me that the flowering trees I'd seen everywhere since I arrived were called jacarandas. I loved their purple blossoms. The pink flowering bushes were called bougainvillea. Two of the sisters, one African and the other a white Zimbabwean invited me to come with them to visit their Shona mission stations at Chisiwasa and Drifontein, southwest of Harare. The sisters and I piled into their late model Land Rover that was sparkling clean and drove 4 hours from Harare to Chisiwasa. Both sisters exuded enthusiasm about their mission to give young people a good education, a chance to choose a profession, and maybe qualify for the University. They both taught at the boarding schools there. The sisters lived on the grounds with the students and acted as both their teachers and their guardians. In these formal, British-style boarding schools, the students wore uniforms; white shirts and pleated skirts for the girls; gray pants, white shirts, and neckties for the boys. Everyone wore boaters: straw hats with a short round brim. The school, built of cement blocks, had highly polished poured cement floors. Every classroom opened onto a wide veranda that surrounded each building. Jacaranda trees, bougainvillea bushes, palm trees, and other exotic looking plants grew everywhere on the landscaped grounds. Zimbabwe was full of surprises and not at all what I had imagined it would be. When the bell rang for class changes, neatly dressed students poured out of their classrooms and into the hallways. The sisters asked me to sit in on a few of the senior students' classes. The students peppered me with questions about life in America, especially about how teenagers lived. Having taught at two high schools, I knew a lot about the ways of American teenagers. They found my accent very amusing and spent a good deal of our time trying to mimic it. The sisters asked me to speak to the teachers about my life in America as well as our team's plan to go to Binga. No one understood why I wanted to go to such a remote and primitive place as Binga.

The sisters took me aside after my conversation with the teachers, "Michael, why don't you stay here with us. We need a priest, and you would be perfect for the students."

I told them I didn't think my bishop or Marge would be happy about that. I did the same thing for the students and teachers in Drifontein. After two nights I hitched a ride back to Harare with another sister. I didn't feel any closer to learning about mission life or what a missionary did.

On February 19, almost two weeks after I arrived, I said Mass at the Cathedral of the Sacred Heart in the center of Harare. It felt like having Mass at the Cathedral in Toledo. This gothic building, constructed in 1890 with two tall towers, stained glass windows, high ceilings, a long nave with pews, and an elevated sanctuary was one of the few remaining British Colonial-era buildings left in Harare. After Mass, I returned to the convent for lunch and then wandered around the convent buildings, bored and wondering what to do next. Marge's words rang in my ears, "Do a little exploring on your own." I didn't know what to explore. All of the sisters were either sleeping or out visiting someone on this particular Sunday afternoon. I found myself walking down a deserted part of the convent on my way back to my room when I heard one of the sisters call out,

"There he is!" She was leading two women down the long, dark hall. When they got to me, she said, "This is Father Mike."

The two women turned out to be an Italian doctor and a Scottish nurse who had been to my Mass at the cathedral and wanted me to come with them.

The Italian doctor asked me, "What are you doing right now?"

"Nothing," I said.

"Then you are coming with us. We have a little shopping to do. We'll be back in an hour. Pack a bag!"

"Yes Ma'am."

I rushed back to my room excited to be getting out of the convent, stuffed a few things into a small suitcase, and after 45 minutes walked out to the front of the buildings. A short time later I heard a roar and then saw a Land Rover covered in dirt and dust careening down the street. It screeched to a halt right in front of me and out tumbled the Scottish nurse who took my bag, threw it on top of the shopping, shoved me into the back seat and crawled in next to me.

"We've got to get moving," she said in a thick Scottish accent. "We've got to get back to Mutoko before it gets dark. Only one headlight works on this thing."

The Land Rover groaned under the load. It took 3 hours to get from Harare to Mutoko, which is in the foothills of the Eastern Highlands of Zimbabwe. Two Canadians, two Italians, the nurse and I sat crammed in the vehicle, along with all of the groceries they purchased to take back to their remote mission station. I didn't mind sitting next to this pretty Scottish nurse. I felt like they liberated me from the confines of the convent complex. The Dominican sisters were kind, but they weren't that much fun. This group laughed and told stories the whole way out to the mission.

As soon as we arrived someone yelled, "Happy Hour!"

Beer and wine flowed the rest of the evening. Their bush mission consisted of a small hospital with a few exam rooms and two large wards, one for men and the other for women. Twenty beds, full of patients, lined each wall. The school consisted of four large classrooms each containing a few desks which students shared, a blackboard, and a few books. Most of the students wore gray shorts and shirts, the uniform for the school, but their outfits looked like they'd come from Goodwill. There were no "boaters" here. There was a veranda around the school made of tin sheeting and held up by a mixture of metal poles and tree trunks. White paint peeled from the walls inside and out. Students shared their textbooks and spent a good deal of time "reciting." Now I understood that bush school meant "primitive." Between classes, students poured out of the classrooms yelling and shouting. Even with only five or ten minutes between classes, a game of soccer would break out on the dusty school grounds, the boys kicking a ball made of a plastic sack stuffed with old rags. A teacher would ring a hand bell, and in a minute everything was quiet again.

Back at the house, every evening someone would yell, "happy hour," and the drinks appeared. An old refrigerator made ice sporadically, so the "missionaries" rationed it out to cool our adult beverages.

During one happy hour, the Scottish nurse looked at me and said, "Why in the world did you become a priest?"

I didn't fit her picture of how a priest acted. I had ducked this question for years. I mumbled something lame, "I was lying face down on a church floor, and the bishop zapped me." They all fell off their chairs laughing. I felt right at home with them. I stayed there for three days. During the day the Scottish nurse showed me around the hospital and the school. She tried to convince me to dump Marge and stay there.

"We need a young priest like you to be with the children," she said.

The offer was enticing, and this time I hated to decline.

A few days later we rode to the bus station in their beaten-up Land Rover.

"There is a bus that will take you right to Harare," the Italian doctor told me. "It will be a good experience for you."

Whenever anyone said the words "this will be good for you," it usually meant something unpleasant was about to happen. Upon arrival at the bus terminal, I was astonished to see the crowd of people waiting; getting onto buses, and getting off buses. Women in colorful flowing robes, most with baskets full of clothes, or food balanced on their heads, and always with a few children trailing behind or clinging to their skirts crammed the terminal. Men were standing in separate groups talking and laughing. How would I ever find my bus in this chaos, I wondered?

The Scottish nurse took me to buy a ticket and then showed me where to wait. "You're sure you don't want to stay with us a while longer?"

"No thank you," I told her. But I didn't mean it. She walked backed to the Land Rover, and they drove away, leaving behind a plume of dark smoke. Ten minutes later a big green bus rumbled into the station and pulled up right next to me. This bus was nothing like the luxury coach Marge and I rode on from Hwange. Luggage was already stacked and tied down on its roof. It looked top-heavy to me. It was painted a dark green and looked like it had been in service for decades. We waited for passengers to get off and then those of us headed for Harare swarmed forward like bees trying to push into their hive. The driver patiently took tickets, greeted everyone, and gave me a look of astonishment when he saw me.

Then he smiled and said, "Welcome aboard," as if he were welcoming me into first class.

I felt a little uneasy at first, being the only white guy. People kept packing into the bus and onto the bench seats. I found a window seat and tried to look unobtrusive. People soon filled the aisle and all at once the diesel engine belched out black smoke and the bus lurched forward onto the road. Passengers loaded and unloaded at every little town and village. Stuff packed the roof. Stuff filled the baggage compartment underneath. Stuff lay in the aisle. But everyone seemed happy and chatty and full of fun. I had a different picture of people in Africa, more like the film of a refugee camp I had watched before I left home; people looking more beaten down and haggard. These people were enjoying themselves, which was not at all what I had imagined. The big green bus pulled into a little store in each small town, where people waited to board it for Harare. At each stop, women rushed up to the bus with food or soft drinks to sell. They moved down the side of the bus calling out to passengers in their local language, Shona, the food and drink they sold in baskets balanced on their heads. At one stop, one of the women caught sight of me sitting there on the bus in my window seat, and we stared at each other for a moment. Then she burst out laughing at the shock of seeing a white guy on the bus and called to her friends to come over to see me. I realized that my efforts at being unobtrusive weren't working very well, and rather than being invisible I was becoming the center of attention. A few of my fellow passengers bought me a drink and something to eat. I felt grateful for their generosity. After ninety minutes we rolled into Harare and I made my way back to my room in the convent.

A few days later Marge arrived in Harare with her passport. Julitta, our third teammate, landed on February 26. What a difference between these two ladies! Marge's focus and determination contrasted with Julitta' easy going and relaxed nature. But both Marge and Julitta were always ready for some fun. I was so glad our little family was now complete. Differences aside, we all shared the same challenge at this moment: to get to Johannesburg to buy a Land Rover. But first, we needed travel visas from the South African Embassy. The Dominicans told me not to declare my occupation as a "priest." The South African government considered priests as troublemakers because apartheid still raged there. "Declare your occupation as 'teacher,'" one sister said. The Bishop in Hwange arranged a meeting for us with a gentleman who lived in Johannesburg and sold Land Rovers. The trip to South Africa also gave me the opportunity to visit yet another of my German cousins, Sr. Robert, a Dominican missionary sister from a convent in Schlehdorf, Bavaria. It took over a week for the visas to come back, which meant more waiting around. What a contrast to the life I left behind at the Cathedral in Toledo, where I rarely got a day off. Everything took so much longer here. And no one seemed to be in a hurry to do anything. A week later we boarded our plane to Johannesburg. After we had landed and deplaned, the white passengers went into one terminal, and the Africans went into another. We followed the white crowd. I had never experienced such blatant racism before. Eventually, we got our luggage and met a Dominican Sister who came to meet us. Johannesburg looked like Chicago or Miami. There were tall buildings, sidewalks full of pedestrians, and buses, taxis, and lots of traffic on the streets. Just like the convent in Harare, the convent in Johannesburg was a haven of quiet and peace in the midst of all of this noise. But South Africa felt like an angry, mean place. I hated seeing "Whites Only" signs everywhere; on the buses, at the beach, and on the drinking fountains.

On March 1, we took a train for East London to meet up with my cousin Sr. Robert, with whom my mother had been corresponding for years. My mother loved writing letters and over many years she connected with my father's German cousins some of whom still lived in Bavaria and others who had become missionaries and moved to South Africa. I met and stayed with many of the Bavarian clan while I studied in Rome, and now I looked forward to meeting Sr. Robert. The train ride took 22 hours. At that time in South Africa, men and women couldn't be together on the train, so Marge and Julitta rode in the women's coach while I rode with the men. We saw each other in the dining car for meals. Sr. Robert met us at the train station in East London. She told us the drive to the convent would take over two hours and warned us about lions and wild animals. We locked the doors and kept our arms in the car. Five minutes later, when we arrived at the convent, she laughed and laughed at how gullible we were! East London is a port city on the Indian Ocean with over 750,000 residents. During our time there, we visited deserted beaches on the Indian Ocean. We picked mushrooms in a forest and played scrabble, Sr. Robert's favorite game. We visited the townships where the Africans lived and commuted to their jobs as domestics for white families or other jobs that no white person wanted. The disparity between the way the whites lived and the way the blacks lived shocked and frightened us. Zimbabwe had abolished apartheid a few years earlier and was taking strides to create a country where blacks and whites could coexist peacefully. Getting a glimpse into this way of life gave me a better insight into just what these countries and their people were experiencing. Sr. Robert's tours offered me another piece of the missionary orientation I needed.

We left Sr. Robert and boarded our train back to Johannesburg on March 6, and connected with the gentleman who arranged the purchase of our Land Rover the following day. I enjoyed driving for the first time in months. The Land Rover handled like a dump truck. The diesel engine roared as it lumbered into gear. It was very different from the yellow VW bug I had driven from Tiffin to Toledo, and now I also had to get used to driving on the left side of the road. There were a few hairy moments when I turned this big vehicle right into oncoming traffic.

On March 8, Marge, Julitta, and I rumbled up the highway out of Johannesburg headed for Zimbabwe. We loved having our own wheels and we drove for two days through stunning landscapes of mountains and savannahs on our way to Bulawayo.

I began to realize that these experiences provided me with the orientation to Africa and mission life that I missed before I left Toledo. In a little over three weeks, I had visited a good deal of Zimbabwe, seen different missions, ridden on an African bus, visited South Africa, and had experienced the vast difference between life in the city and life in the bush. Without any planning on my part, higher forces had arranged my whole orientation. Little did I suspect that there was much more than this planned for me in the coming years.

We spent two nights in Bulawayo shopping and loading our new vehicle with groceries and supplies for our next destination, Kariangwe Mission, among the Tongas with whom we planned to live and work. The streets of Bulawayo teemed with people. At one corner we waited with a crowd of pedestrians to cross. When the light changed, I stepped off the curb and a bicyclist knocked me off my feet and flat onto my back. Everyone stopped. The African riding the bike looked down at me. I looked up at him. Time froze. Then I noticed blood seeping from a rip in the knee of my pants. I laid there helpless. Marge took charge of the situation.

"Are you Ok?" She reached down and helped me to my feet.

We walked to the other side of the street. My knee oozed blood. Marge took a quick look at the bloody tear, "You'll be okay. Let's go over there and get something to eat."

We walked into a restaurant, sat in a booth, ordered lunch, and waited. My knee started to throb. After 20 minutes, the waitress brought a heaping tray of french-fries and hamburgers. She served me two of everything because I said "me too" when Marge and Julitta ordered burgers and fries.

I looked at Marge and Julitta and said, "Blood is dripping down my leg and into my socks. Let's go back to the convent."

At the convent, the sisters treated my knee with some medicated powder and a gauze wrapping. I had skinned it pretty badly and the deep cuts continued to ooze. Before we left the next day, the sisters worked on my knee again, changing the dressing and giving me more gauze and medicated powder. On March 10 the three of us arrived back in Hwange.

The next morning, Bishop Prieto told me that he wanted to get to know our new teammate, Julitta.

"Michael, I want to take you and the other sisters to lunch."

He drove the old white Renault to the sister's convent where we picked up Marge and Julitta and then he drove us up to the Baobab Hotel for lunch. We sat under an ancient baobab tree high on a bluff overlooking the vast savannah that surrounded Hwange. We ate fried chicken and fries and told the bishop about our adventures in Harare, Johannesburg, and East

London. After lunch, we drove back to his house. As he parked the car in front of the long veranda and switched off the engine, he ordered us to stay in the car. We watched in horror as he grabbed a shovel leaning against a wall and began to beat a huge snake coiled on the porch. It was like watching a Spanish Santa Clause in a kick boxing match with a snake. He was all over the front porch shouting and swinging at the creature.

When I asked him if he needed help, he shouted, "Stay in the car. I have glasses to protect my eyes from this spitting cobra. If the venom gets in your eyes, it will blind you."

I stayed put and watched him shovel the snake corpse into the bush.

I felt like a child learning how to walk and talk. From the surprising decision of the discernment team to my mission visits while I waited for Marge, my lessons came from unexpected sources: a wild Italian doctor, women at the bus stop, a Spanish bishop, a cousin from Germany, an African on a bike. And this was only the beginning.

Chapter 4

Kariangwe March 1984

Marge, Julitta, and I couldn't wait to get started with our missionary work which meant that we had to learn the Tonga language and culture. We planned to do this at an established mission in the area called Kariangwe. We would spend as much time there as we needed until we felt comfortable enough with the language and the culture to move out on our own. Kariangwe's mission territory covered about 300 square miles. We would inherit the northern half of the area that included three established outstations when we were ready. We planned to take our first baby steps into life as missionaries at Kariangwe. I felt a little more comfortable now that I received an "orientation" to mission life from the lovely Scottish nurse, and the Italian doctor at their mission in Mutoko. Fr. Joseph gave us driving directions to Kariangwe. He drew us a map filled with landmarks like "the big red rock," "the Baobab tree," or "the road right after the fork." He wanted to come with us to make sure we got there okay.

"Don't worry about us," Marge said, "we're not babies."

The next day after 7:00 AM Mass and breakfast with the Bishop, I fired up our new Landrover, and we took off to find Kariangwe. The three of us sat on the front bench seat as we roared out of town. We turned south onto the "super highway" toward Bulawayo driving past a game reserve that covered hundreds of square miles called Hwange National Park. About a third of the way from Hwange to Bulawayo we found the turnoff for the road to Kamitivi which consisted of two paved tracks. A vehicle alone on the road drove on both tracks, but when another vehicle approached, each one moved off to its left, making sure that one wheel was on one track while the other wheel rode on the shoulder. I found it a little tricky moving onto one track, allowing the oncoming Land Rover to pass and then maneuvering back onto both tracks all the while maintaining my speed. The Land Rover was not that stable or agile. All of the other drivers seemed more comfortable driving in this way and in a few instances I barely got out of the way while they sped past, one hand on the wheel and the other waving out the window. My hands gripped the wheel tightly while Marge shouted directions from the front passenger seat.

"Land Rover approaching ahead. Get over, Mike."

Julitta, I believe, wanted to get down on her knees to pray. The road passed through a steep gorge outside of Kamitivi. I white-knuckled the steering wheel as I guided the Land Rover down the steep grade that ended in a narrow bridge spanning a wide, deep river. I felt relieved as I drove across the bridge and we marveled at the rock cliffs that rose hundreds of feet high from the edge of the water. The road climbed straight up the gorge once I crossed the bridge and we crawled up the other side in first gear. In future months I would roar down one side, speed across the bridge and make the up-side trip in second gear, but at this moment, I didn't yet possess that kind of nerve.

Once we passed through the little village of Kamitivi, the road turned into sand, complete with what everyone called "corrugations," or continuous small ridges crossing the road. I drove fast enough to float over them – a sandy hydroplaning. A mushroom cloud of dust rose behind us as we zoomed along. Marge, unhappy with how fast we were going, shouted out a "slow down" warning, but as I slowed the Land Rover began to vibrate. Then she'd yell, "speed up." And in this way, we moved down the road. "Slow down." "Speed up."

The villages we passed looked much different than the ones we'd seen when the sisters took me out to their boarding schools near Harare. Here the mud adobe flaked off the side of the rondavels in large chunks, exposing the wooden poles of the walls. The grass thatch for roofing was much thinner. I began to feel more comfortable driving the enormous Landrover after having to shift from track to track and driving through the gorge. But now dashing along over this sandy road I could feel the big vehicle wanted to fishtail. After a while I drifted into a driver's stupor when Marge's voice jarred me to attention,

"Stop! There's the turn off for Kariangwe."

I stomped on the brakes, and the Land Rover slid past the turnoff and began to fishtail, almost sending us off the road. I was surprised at how little it took to make such a large vehicle slide on these sandy roads. A few hundred yards later we came to a stop. I see-sawed back and forth in the middle of the road until we made an "about face" and then drove to the Kariangwe turn-off. Our broad, sandy road now narrowed into a single lane. We entered into a semi-forested area that felt like a jungle. I found myself navigating the Land Rover around hairpin turns and along narrow, mountain-like passes where one side of the road dropped into a deep ravine. Marge poked her head out the passenger side window telling me how close we were to the edge.

I picked my way along for 45 minutes with Marge yelling out, "A foot," "six inches" and finally, "plenty of room."

As the road flattened out, Marge pulled in her head, and we all relaxed. More villages appeared along the way, more people walking, and all at once we were at the mission compound.

After six hours of driving, we rolled into the mission just as the sun was setting. We felt relieved that we did not have to drive that narrow road in the dark. We passed by a store, a school, a hospital, a church, a convent, and stopped in front of the priests' house. Tonga rondavels surrounded this sprawling little outpost of whitewashed buildings. We felt proud that we made it all that way on our own. Pulling up to the priests' house, Fr. Joshua and Br. Manolo both from Spain and Fr. Ananias, a Shona priest stationed at Kariangwe, stood there smiling and waving. The Spanish sisters, who ran the hospital and the school, ran out of their house to greet us. They welcomed us with hugs, handshakes, and lots of cheek-kissing. I felt exhausted. We had made it to the end of the first segment of our journey. Kariangwe became our home for the next four months.

The mission lacked electricity and hot water. Drinking water came from a spring where Br. Manolo filled jugs every few days. A long porch ran the length of the house. My room consisted of a bed, a dresser, a small table, a desk and a chair - more like a cell than a room.

It was August 1983 when I had put my name first into the hat to come to Zimbabwe. Now, in March 1984, I was living on a mission. Seven months earlier I had worked at the Cathedral in Toledo, lived in a mansion, taught high school kids, and enjoyed evenings with friends. Now, I was living on a bush station with few amenities and no friends. I felt lost and confused. It brought back vivid memories of my ordination day, August 7, 1977. Ordination day culminated 12 years of study and preparation, but it turned into a disaster for me. I laid on the floor alone in the middle of the church on that steamy Saturday afternoon wondering what I was doing there. It was a question I still asked myself over and over again. Bishop Donovan ordained me in my parish church, St. Patrick of Heatherdowns. At the end of Mass, the bishop announced to everyone my first assignment.

"Fr. Schoenhofer is assigned to St. Mary's Church in Tiffin, Ohio. He will report there on Wednesday."

The organ struck up the final song, and I turned leading the procession out of the church. As I marched down the aisle, smiling at everyone on the outside, on the inside, I felt sick, because I knew I had just made a terrible mistake. As I walked out of the church, the first person to greet me was my old girlfriend, my last love. She hugged me, kissed me on the cheek tearfully, and then disappeared. My first assignment, Tiffin Ohio, was her hometown. The Divine Comedian should get an Emmy, I thought, I just married the wrong girl! For the next few days, I found myself weeping and saying over and over to myself, "What a damned fool!" Then I told myself, I'll have to suck it up now for the rest of my life. Within a week of my arrival in Tiffin, the Chancellor of the Diocese, the Bishop's second in command, called to tell me that the Bishop forgot to inform me that part of my assignment involved teaching five classes a day, three days a week at the Catholic high school, Tiffin Calvert. Great, I thought, here's another thing I feel unprepared for and don't want to do. The new associate priest at the neighboring parish, St. Joseph's, was a classmate, recently ordained, who welcomed me to town and then said,

"Mike, since St. Mary always runs the religion classes for kids who didn't go to Catholic schools in the past, I don't want to change that. You can take on the program."

I was speechless. That program started in less than three weeks. Classes at Calvert started in less than two weeks. I didn't even feel comfortable saying Mass yet. My mind reeled. But the assignment in Tiffin St. Mary's lasted for almost three years. In that time, I grew to love my pastor, Fr. Shanahan, who treated me like a son and who felt so sorry for me the first year that he gave me an extra week's vacation. He and I worked up a song and dance routine for gatherings of parishioners or teachers at the school.

He told me, "Let's use the name - 'Shan and Shane, We Entertain.'"

I must have looked puzzled.

"You know," he said, "Shan for Shanahan and Shane for Schoenhofer: Shan and Shane."

He was very proud of that name and even came up with straw hats and canes for the performance. I loved the people of the parish, and the kids I taught at Calvert. But I never felt at home. After three years, the

Bishop assigned me to the Cathedral in Toledo where I taught high school sophomores at Central Catholic. I loved the people and the kids there too, but I felt something missing like I was doing time. Now, years later at Kariangwe, life settled into a routine. And I was still doing time, just in a different place. I celebrated Mass with Fr. Joshua and Fr. Ananias every morning at 7:00 AM. Then we all ate breakfast together. Afterward, I studied Tonga for a few hours, and then all three of us joined Fr. Joshua for our daily Tonga language lesson. I studied for another 2 hours. We ate lunch around 1:00 followed by a siesta. I studied for another few hours in the afternoon. Julitta, Marge and I met in the early evening for "team time" which entailed talking about how we felt about our transition to living out in the bush, learning the language, and the next steps we needed to take to get our mission established in Binga. Marge wanted to make sure Julitta and I were adjusting to this new life.

"It's going to take some time to learn to live with the poor. When I used to live on the streets with the people, we sat around a big fire in the evening, and we all ate one bowl of soup. You two should be happy you have a bed." Then she'd look at my long face and say, "Buck up, Mike."

Marge didn't have much time for moping around or whining. In the evening we all sat in the lounge around a bright gaslight and either read a book or made small talk about the day. There wasn't much to chat about since I wasn't doing much. I felt isolated and lonelier than when I had lived in the parish. A deep depression began to settle in, and I thought about ways that I could escape the monotony, boredom, and lack of close and intimate friendships. Many of my thoughts included self-injury. My head was not in a safe space.

Chapter 5

Kariangwe St. Patrick's Day 1984

We celebrated St. Patrick's Day a week after we arrived in Kariangwe. I don't believe that Fr. Joshua, Brother Manolo, or Fr. Ananias had any particular devotion to the Irish saint, but we convinced them this might be a good evening for a party. Br. Manolo organized a big meal, and I contributed a bottle of bourbon for the occasion. After "happy hour" we moved from the living room to the dining room to eat. A few minutes after we sat down to eat the front door banged open behind me, and I watched Fr. Joshua jump to his feet with his arms raised over his head. When I turned around, I saw the school headmaster standing in the doorway with two men behind him. As the men pushed him into the room, I saw that these guys were carrying assault rifles. The next minute we all stood with our arms up. The men ordered us out of the house to the front of the mission. We filed out of the dining room, through the lounge and out into the darkness in front of the mission.

"Lay down here," the gunmen ordered, "with your faces in the sand."

We all laid face down in the sand except for Brother Manolo who refused to put his head down. I lay there wondering what it would feel like to have a bullet shot into my head. I imagined an initial burning sensation, and then, darkness. I was between Fr. Joshua and Br. Manolo. Ananias, Marge, and Julitta were laying in the sand at the other end of the line. Manolo rested his chin on his hands, elbows in the sand, and glared at the man with the gun. I don't know what unnerved me more, the men with the assault rifles or Manolo's stare.

"Give me your watches," the gunman ordered.

We all surrendered our watches and anything of value. One guy stationed himself in the house and called us in one by one where we surrendered anything he thought was valuable from our rooms. When he pointed at me with his rifle to come into the house, I felt a little wobbly.

The gunmen said, "Show me your room."

I felt his gun on my back as I lead him down the hallway. He stood in the doorway, and I sat on the bed. He shoved a sack at me,

"Put your valuables here and don't try to hide anything."

I gave him my camera and all of my Zimbabwean money. My hands shook as I handed it over.

He looked at me and said, "I am not going to kill you."

After we had given them our belongings, the gunmen ordered us to get up out of the sand and then marched us through the bush toward the store at the other end of the mission. On the way, they ordered anyone who happened to be outside to join the march. Soon over 20 people were walking single file through the bush to the store. At one point, the gunmen closest to me stepped on a stick that bounced up and hit my leg.

"Sorry about that," he said.

I knew then that I needn't worry anymore about a bullet in my head. When we arrived at the store, the gunmen ordered everyone to grab a bottle of milk and drink it. I suppose at that point since none of us paid for the milk we all became accomplices. Then they locked us into the store and escaped.

Once they had gone everyone started talking, I could hear Spanish, Tonga, Shona, and English. Manolo and Joshua found a key and let us all out. Manolo, more enraged than frightened, ran out of the open doors hunting for the gunmen. Marge found Julitta and I standing in shock in the store and gave us both a big hug.

"Let's get out of here."

We walked together in silence back to the priests' house.

"Let's sit together under this tree for a while. We should feel safe in the shade," Marge said.

We were afraid to go back into the house in case the gunmen came back for a second round. The moon shone so brightly that sitting in the shadow cast by the trees made us feel invisible. Marge had similar frightening experiences in her previous mission assignment, and now I found her mission stories comforting. Marge kept talking to us in a quiet whisper and slowly I began to relax. After half an hour Manolo came back and told us the gunmen were gone. He seemed disappointed that he'd missed a good fight.

"Go to bed," he told us.

We didn't know if the gunmen were common thieves, or if they were Ndebele guerrilla fighters caught up in the ongoing struggle for control of the country. They looked like soldiers to us with their gray fatigues and assault rifles.

The next day, a troop of police officers who had been tracking these guys for the past few weeks arrived at the mission. When we described what happened, they kept apologizing and saying, "Shit!" They had slipped through their fingers again.

Word of the robbery reached Hwange, and the next day Bishop Prieto and Fr. Joseph arrived in their little white Renault to check on us. They stayed for the day looking us over, worried about our state of mind since we'd only just arrived in the country a few months earlier and had only been on our own at the mission for a little over a week. Even by their estimation, this was a traumatic event, and they'd lived here during the war years. My knee injury from being knocked down by the bicyclist in Bulawayo felt terrible. When I looked at it the next morning, red streaks radiated into my thigh from the center of the wound. Lying face down in the sand during the robbery had only worsened the injury. After lunch, I walked over to the hospital to have one of the sisters take a look at it. As I sat in the exam room, I felt feverish and closed my eyes.

The sister taking my blood pressure said, "This is not possible. I can't find your blood pressure."

When I opened my eyes, Joshua and Manolo were standing over me with Marge in the background. At first, I wondered how everyone had gotten there so quickly. Then I realized I had fainted and had fallen off the chair onto the floor of the exam room. Manolo and Joshua grabbed me under the arms and helped me get onto an exam table where I laid under the watchful eye of the sister while Manolo went to get some tea and cookies. I felt better after eating, and Joshua and Manolo guided me back to the priests' house. Once safely in my room, I sat on the bed. Marge stood at the door and glared at me,

"If this ever happens again, please tell me where you are going. I was really worried about you. "

I laid down and wrapped myself in feelings of doom and gloom. The nursing sister told me to stop using the medicated powder. She gave me soap, an antiseptic cream, and rolls of gauze and said,

"Report back here to me every day. I want to make sure this wound is healing."

I was getting a lot of orders.

The Bishop and Fr. Joseph left for Hwange the next morning, and I settled back into the mind-numbing routine of language study. As the days and weeks at Kariangwe passed I continued to feel lost, confused, and alone.

Chapter 6

Kariangwe, Binga, Nakangala March / April 1984

F r. Joshua encouraged us to speak to people in Tonga whenever we had the opportunity. He taught us to greet someone by clapping our hands together and saying, "Mwabuka. Mwabuka bieni?" (Good Morning. How are you?) So whenever I took a walk and came upon someone, I said,

"Mwabuka. Mwabuka bieni?"

The person I addressed would stop and say something to me in Tonga. Not knowing what they meant, I replied, "Twalumba." (Thank you.)

The person looked puzzled and would reply, "Twalumba" and walk away.

After a few of these encounters, I asked Joshua to teach me how to say, "I have no idea what you said. Can you speak more slowly?" I became discouraged at my slow pace of learning Tonga until I realized that the school children were all learning English at the mission school. I could speak to them in Tonga and, when they replied in Tonga, I could ask them in English to speak more slowly, and to translate what they said. What a relief! I came to the realization that although I was 32 years old in the USA, in Kariangwe I was a child. I could only speak in simple declarative sentences. The children became my teachers. The school children thought this was the funniest thing and whenever they saw me walking, crowds of them would come over to see what I would say. It became a game. I learned something new and then waited for a group of children to gather. Then I'd launch my new Tonga phrase. When the adults saw the kids laughing at me, they'd come over to find out what was so funny. Pretty soon I was stringing together little sentences. When I'd ask the children what they said, they'd all answer together like they were reciting in class. I slowly began to feel more comfortable trying out words and sentences. Studying in my room became a lot more fun as I constructed and practiced little phrases and paragraphs to say to the children. They would correct me, but they understood me too. These little guys were giving me confidence. I needed this lightening up.

Julitta, Marge, and I began to go with Fr. Joshua and Fr. Ananias to the mission stations they planned to turn over to us. Two weeks after the robbery, the three of us took our first trip with Fr. Joshua to Binga, the site for our primary mission and where we planned to build our houses. It was starting to get a bit cooler now that we were heading into Fall. It was hard to get used to the seasons in the Southern Hemisphere where summer was winter and winter was summer. Because of Binga's elevation, it was either stinking hot or just really hot. We were too close to the equator to feel any temperature change in the seasons. Binga sat on the edge of a huge lake that spanned almost the entire border between Zimbabwe and Zambia. Lake Kariba was created by damming the Zambezi River in the 1960's to provide hydro-electric power. We drove past the new government center, a few cement block buildings, then along a stretch of sandy road with a few homes scattered along the high bluff overlooking the lake and finally into the little town with a store and a school. We pulled into the schoolyard where people had already gathered for Mass. Every single man, woman, and child came out to greet Fr. Joshua and us, shook our hands, and said, "Mwabuka." The hand-shaking alone took 20 minutes. Then we walked into the classroom, set up the teacher's desk as an altar, sat down and waited for the drummers to begin the first song. At the first drum beat, everyone stood and began to sway. Marge, Julitta, and I joined in the singing and dancing even though we didn't know the words or the melody. Marge and Julitta sat with the women while I sat in front with Fr. Joshua. Both of them were beaming. Two hours later the service finished and Fr. Joshua drove us back to Kariangwe.

On the long drive back to Kariangwe, we were excited about our first encounter with the people of Binga. A month later we went to Binga on our own for the first time. I said Mass and preached in Tonga from a written sermon.

At the end of April, we all went with Fr. Ananias to a more remote mission station called Nakangala. The trip took four hours over corrugated, sandy roads. By the time we arrived the sun had already set, and it was beginning to get dark. Our accommodations consisted of two huts made of mud with grass thatched roofs. They looked terrible to me with mud peeling off the walls and the thatching thin in many places. As soon as we got there, many people from the nearby villages came to greet us. Everything stopped as we went around the whole group shaking each one's hand and giving the traditional "Mwabuka" greeting. Once we greeted everyone, we could unpack our vehicles. The children kept coming from the villages as word spread of our arrival. They watched, wide-eyed as we put our cots, mosquito nets, sleeping bags, and clothes into the huts. Despite the ramshackle appearance of the huts, I felt comfortable and safe under the mosquito netting. At night we heard singing in the nearby villages and the occasional trumpet of an elephant from the adjoining game reserve. Images from the Tarzan movies of my youth lulled me to sleep!

We celebrated Mass in the late morning the next day. No one had watches, so in order to schedule a time to meet, people pointed to the place in the sky where the sun would be when they wanted to start something. I didn't know East from West on a good day, and pointed my hand toward the horizon to the South or the North. People looked at me puzzled until someone figured out the time I was trying to tell and pointed his hand in the proper direction at the right level. Everyone laughed and shook their heads in agreement. The people had built the church in Nakangala years ago in the style of their own homes; wooden poles, with a grass thatch roof and mud wall. The wall stopped halfway to the roof. Inside, the pews consisted of limbs of trees stuck into the ground with a cross piece for a seat. Anywhere from 30 – 40 people gathered for Mass on Sunday in this cool, breezy space. They loved the chance to get together, and at the beginning of a song everyone stood up to dance. The rhythmic swaying and clapping along with up to five drummers accompanied the intricate harmonies of each song. The older women ululated (a high pitched falsetto-like yodel) to emphasize an individual verse. They practiced the songs in their villages in the evening around the fire where they learned these incredible harmonies. If the congregation liked a particular song, they might sing it over again, and sometimes sing it a third time because they had so much fun with the drumming and the dancing and the harmonies. Mass lasted at least two hours. No one had any place better to be than right there together. Why rush? At first everyone called me Bafada (a Tonganized word from the English word "father") Mike. Later they changed Mike to a Tonga name - Syamuunda; the Tonga translation of Schoenhofer, which means in German - "a beautiful gardener." The Tongas translated that into - "the one who keeps the field." I felt like an adopted Tonga child with my new name - Syamuunda. I liked it.

Entering into the rhythmic swaying of the dance, the complex beat of the drums, and the repetitive melody became an experience of timelessness and absolute unity with those around me. My individual personality fell away as I entered into the song and felt surrounded by the music, the drumming, and the singing. It felt peaceful even in the midst of the heat and the poverty. The Tongas smiled and laughed as they encouraged me to continue to sing and dance with them. I felt like the child that they were teaching how to live in this stark simplicity, without the trappings and illusions of western life.

I depended on the school children to teach me their language and culture. Everyone I met accepted me. What a gift! They were giving me a reprieve from my self-imposed life sentence of "doing time" perhaps. The Tonga children helped me to take my first steps in finding happiness. I was stumbling into it. These encounters with the children and the people provided brief moments of light and peace in the midst of the pervasive loneliness I had experienced since that ordination day in August seven years earlier. I didn't understand then how much I needed these people.

People loved going to confession before Mass. Everyone lined up to tell me their sins. Given the state of my Tonga, I had no idea what they were saying. I think they knew that. Maybe that's why my line was a lot longer than the one for Fr. Ananias!

After each of our trips Marge, Julitta, and I got together to talk about our experience. While I was busy in the front of the congregation leading the service and teaching, Marge and Julitta sat with the women either outside our huts or in our little church. The women and children loved teaching them new Tonga words and dance steps. In the past, only priests came out to celebrate Mass. Marge and Julitta brought a whole new dimension to these visits as they laughed and talked and danced with the women. Now the Tonga women had European women they could talk to and they loved it. Soon the women invited Marge and Julitta to learn how to cook nsima (a stiff mash made with white corn flour that was the mainstay of every meal) with them. The Tonga men and women gathered separately to talk. Marge found this difficult as she felt cut off from the discussions the men were having with me which she felt were more important. Later it would be the women who were instrumental in keeping people alive during a terrible drought. Occasionally she broke away from the women and joined me with the men. Marge kept track of our plans and ideas in a little notebook she always carried in a big bag. She would use her notes for our discussions every day at "team time." I was glad she had these notes because I was so busy talking to the men, celebrating Mass, or hearing confessions that I couldn't remember everything we talked about. By July, we couldn't wait to move to Binga and continue our Tonga learning on our own but first we needed a place to live in Binga. Things were about to get more interesting.

(Photo: The Baobab Hotel grounds)

Chapter 7

Binga August 1984

———————

In the months before we moved Marge, Julitta, and I made the 2-hour drive from Kariangwe to Binga once a week to look for somewhere to live. The village plan for Binga identified a barren stretch of sandy bush covered in scrub as the site for a future housing compound. Still not accustomed to how slowly things moved in Zimbabwe, we picked out two plots right under the only two trees in the area. The bureaucratic wheels turned slower than we thought. We scheduled an appointment every week with local government officials to try and accelerate the process. We needed a permit to buy the two plots of land we wanted. Marge found the whole process frustrating which fired up her determination to get this done. A few months into the process we visited with an official in the new government center in Binga in a row of unpainted cement block buildings. As soon as we walked into the building, a receptionist greeted us and hurried back to inform him of our arrival. He invited us into his office, his desk stacked with important-looking papers.

"Come in. Come in. Glad to see you. Please sit down."

He always looked so happy that we just knew that he must have some news.

"Would you like a cup of tea?"

Trying not to show our anxiety as well as trying to fit into the relaxed pace of this culture, we accepted.

"How are things progressing with your mission?"

Marge did the talking for the team. "We are learning Tonga and visiting the area getting to know people," she said.

"Ah! Excellent," he said.

And we chit-chatted in this way until the tea and cookies arrived. Then after what seemed a reasonable amount of time to us, Marge asked,

"Is there any news about our permits from Harare?"

"No, unfortunately, we have not heard anything yet. The wheels turn slowly there these days."

He shook his head sadly. We finished our tea, got into our Land Rover and drove back to Kariangwe.

"Two hours of driving, an hour of chit chat, all for what we could have found out in less than a minute," Marge was fuming.

This scene occurred over and over again. After weeks of this, Marge decided to end the niceties. Now when we arrived, Julitta and I waited in the Land Rover while Marge marched into the building. A few minutes later she emerged shaking her head and climbed back into the Land Rover completely exasperated. She flicked her hand in the "Let's get the hell out of here gesture," and we roared out of the parking lot. We wanted to move to Binga but couldn't get a place to live. Months went by with no building permits from Harare. We knew that the official did want to help us, but as a low-level bureaucrat in this remote area, he couldn't do much to hurry the process along.

On one of our visits to Binga, I saw another white guy walking near the government offices. He was short, stout, and had a white beard. Yes.

He looked like Santa Claus in shorts. I walked up to him and introduced myself.

"I'm Fr. Mike, a missionary here."

"Glad to meet Y'all. I'm Tom Coffee. Call me T. Coffee. Get it T. Coffee?" He laughed and knuckled me in the ribs.

I asked him, "Where are you from?"

"Louisville, Kentucky," he said.

He told me he'd arrived in the country over 20 years ago. He came to work for the government of Southern Rhodesia under the white rule and now worked for the new government of Zimbabwe. But he seemed happy enough about the change and liked living in the bush. "Nobody bothers you a-way out here," he said. I told him about our predicament with the government and getting our permits.

"Y'all are going to be waiting a long time," he said, "things are slower now than before. And I reckon they were pretty slow then. But I like slow." He went on, "But if Y'all are looking for a place to live, I've got a place to rent right on the lake."

Now, this seemed pretty promising. We could move to Binga, live in a little rental property and instead of a two-hour drive from Kariangwe we could go to the government office every day if we wanted.

"Can you show us your place now?"

He said he had a long lunch break coming up and he'd take us out to see the place then. We agreed to meet in an hour. I couldn't wait to tell Marge and Julitta my news. I went back to the Land Rover and told them about T. Coffee's rental that we could see in about an hour. Marge's face lit up.

"Maybe we can move out on our own," she said.

We drove around looking for a place to eat the lunch we brought with us from Kariangwe. We found a spot in the shade of a tree with a beautiful view of the lake. At noon we met Tom and followed him into a different part of Binga. We drove on the sandy road past the future compound where we hoped to build our houses, down a steep hill toward the lake and then along the lake shore for about a mile. The road took a sharp turn to the left and to our astonishment we saw a row of large homes with manicured lawns on a sloping hill that ended on this dirt road. Tucked in between these mansions sat Tom's rental. We drove up a steep driveway and found ourselves in front of a long ranch home built of river rock. This little place had three bedrooms, a kitchen, a great room that opened onto a covered porch that overlooked Lake Kariba. The house was bigger than the entire priests' house in Kariangwe. Tom agreed to rent the house to us until we could get our homes built in the compound. We couldn't believe our luck, living in the lap of luxury in this remote place. Marge was ecstatic. "We can move out of Kariangwe and be on our own."

On August 1 Marge, Julitta, and I packed our Land Rover full of all the stuff we bought in Bulawayo for our new life in Binga, said farewell to the priests and sisters in Kariangwe, and drove out the bush road to Binga. Later that day we moved into Tom's house in Binga. Every few days we drove to the ministry office to check on our building permits and received the same disheartening news. We also began to take over the work of Kariangwe's outstations in Binga, Nakangala, and Kalungwizi. How strange to be living in a beautiful home in the middle of the white settlement with stunning views of the lake, while getting ready to work among the poorest people in Zimbabwe.

The whites built their luxury homes along the lake at the lower end of Binga, while the government workers lived in modest two-bedroom homes in the town center. The Tongas lived in villages surrounding the town. We were in the high rent district of Binga, at least for now. We discovered a beautiful tourist resort 800 yards from T. Coffee's house called the Safari Camp. The resort attracted people who wanted to get away from the hustle and bustle of city life to relax in the bush and take in the beauty of Lake Kariba. The Safari Camp consisted of a store that sold fresh meat, canned vegetables, and bread, a gas station, a restaurant, a long row of cabins, and a large swimming pool all with a stunning view of Lake Kariba. I never imagined such "luxury" so close to where I lived in this remote mission area. In my letters home I downplayed the luxury part of the area and focused on the "hard missionary life" I lived.

Peter Muleya, the church leader for Binga, came from Nakangala. Peter worked for the government and lived in the town center. He spoke excellent English and became a mentor, guide, translator, and teacher of the Tonga culture for us. Peter himself was a Tonga, slim, medium height, with thick black hair. Even here in remote Binga, he always wore a suit and necktie everywhere. He suggested that we start a bible discussion group to get to know people better. That seemed easy enough, and Peter did all the hard work of reaching out to the community leaders in Binga. Peter invited both Shona and Tonga men who worked with him in government service to our gatherings. We talked more about their lives than we did about the Bible. One man told about escaping a lion attack, while another related how hyenas carried off a few children in his village. The conversation often focused on whether their families had enough food, sicknesses like malaria which ravaged the people, or the death of a relative. My training and orientation continued.

I endured long stretches of time when nothing happened. And even though I missed the busyness of my life in Toledo, my students at Central Catholic, the Cathedral Parish, and my family and close friends, I was finally making some new friends and starting to feel useful.

Chapter 8

The Crash August 1984

———————

After three more weeks of regular visits to see the government official, Marge was fed up.

"The only way we are going to get these permits is to go get them ourselves. Pack your bags. We are going to Harare, and I'll take care of this myself."

Julitta and I obeyed. On August 23 we left our rental unit on the lake and took off for Harare. Marge found driving the massive Land Rover difficult.

"I need to keep driving this thing until I get used to it," she said. "I'll take the first shift to Harare."

We left early for the eight-hour trip. If it got too late, we could stop at a hotel in Kariba, at the other end of the lake near the dam wall.

When we set off for Harare that morning, the sun shone brightly with not a cloud in the sky, just like every day in Binga. It only ever rained a few months out of the year. Being the middle of winter, we expected the temperature to rise into the 80's, cool for this area. We drove out of Binga on the sandy roads and turned east toward Nakangala. We felt excited to be exploring a new part of the country. The road wound through a vast game reserve that stretched to the lake and then along the lake for hundreds of miles. Thick forests grew on both sides of the road. No one lived here. The Land Rover rumbled along this section of the road where the shoulder dropped off sharply on either side. Marge seemed more comfortable as she zoomed along leaving a cloud of dust in her wake. As we talked about our plans once we got to Harare, I noticed that the Land Rover had drifted close to the left side of the road. All at once, the left front wheel slipped onto the steeply banked shoulder, and the big white beast of a vehicle began tilting downward toward the forest. Marge tried to get the Land Rover back under control but she overcorrected, and it turned sideways. It slid along for a few yards and then started into a slow roll landing first on its side and then coming to rest on the roof. Everything paused for a moment and then the roof began to buckle. I waited as the Landrover crunched downward and stopped. Marge and I hung from our seat belts which were now suspending us over the roof resting on the ground. Marge looked unconscious. I put my foot down on the roof, unbuckled my seat belt and saw Marge looking around. I helped her out of her seatbelt and then Julitta poked her head up from the back looking a little dazed.

"Hello," she said.

Julitta had gotten thrown around a bit in the back.

We crawled through the vehicle, out the back door, and sat down on the edge of the road. No one spoke. Finally, Julitta said, "At least we're alive."

None of us could look at our Land Rover for a few minutes. We knew we couldn't roll it back onto its tires. It seemed like a giant turtle with its great wheels sticking up in the air. Our beautiful white Land Rover that we had driven all the way from South Africa looked dead. We were in the middle of the game reserve. As we sat there, grateful to be alive and unhurt, we heard the sound of a motor in the distance. Unbelievably, within a few minutes of our wreck, we saw a car coming down the road. I ran out to flag it down, even though it must have been evident that an upside down Land

Rover in the middle of nowhere with three people sitting next to it would need help. The car pulled over.

The driver looked at us, "Are you guys Ok?"

"We're Ok," I said, "but we need some help. You sound American."

"Yup. I'm from Kansas working here for the summer in the tsetse fly control."

There in the middle of nowhere stood four Americans.

"Can you give us a ride to the police station in Nakangala?"

"I'm not supposed to give anyone a ride in this car. It's a government vehicle, and if anyone saw me, I could get into big trouble," he said.

"Look," Marge said, " what is wrong with you? We need help. Drop us off at the police station, and then you can take off. There's no one out here to see you."

He reluctantly agreed. "I can only fit two of you in my car."

Marge turned to Julitta, "you stay here with the car. You've got plenty of food and water. If you see any wild animals, crawl in the car."

This reluctant Kansan drove us 35 miles to the police camp and stopped about a half a mile away. "You'll have to get out here and walk the rest of the way. I can't take a chance on anyone seeing me. Good luck."

Marge and I walked the rest of the way to the police camp and told the officers there about the accident. They agreed to radio to Binga to get us some help. We'd been on our own in Binga for less than four weeks and in the country for only five months, so we had no idea what to do in this situation.

Marge took charge again, "We can't stand around here all our lives. Let's walk back to the main road and see if we can flag someone down to help us."

I tried to convince her not to walk that far since so few vehicles traveled on that road. "We could be standing out there all day," I said.

But she'd already made up her mind, "We've got to do something. We've got to get back to Julitta at least," she said.

So we walked the 2 kilometers back to the main road. I was silent the whole way, seething at the stupidity of this idea. As soon as we got to the main crossroad, a huge truck appeared out of nowhere.

"This is impossible," I said. The driver stopped. We told him our problem.

"Jump in. I can help you. I have to stop at the store in Nakangala to pick up a few things first," he told us.

Marge turned, looked at me, and just smiled. Mercifully she kept her thoughts to herself.

I was mortified and mumbled, "I guess this was a pretty good idea after all."

We climbed into the cab and sat down. The trucker drove us a few miles to the little outpost store and parked his rig. Marge and I found a place to sit in the front of the store and waited. Two hours later, we were still sitting and waiting. Nothing moved fast around here. A local Methodist minister happened along and after hearing the story of our crash agreed to take us back to where Julitta was waiting. We abandoned the truck and went with him. As we drove along another car approached - it was the doctor's wife from Binga, Regine, who had received a message from the police and had driven out to look for us. (Philip, a Sri Lankan doctor, and Regine, a German, were married and worked at the Binga Hospital.) Julitta was sitting next to her in the front seat. Both vehicles stopped in the middle of the road, and we all jumped out and hugged each other, Regine, and even the Methodist Minister. We were so happy to be reunited. Julitta looked sunburned and tired. Once we all finished hugging, Marge said,

"I'll go with the Minister back to the crash site and wait for the truck. Mike, you and Julitta go with Regine to get the police to guard our vehicle overnight in case the truck doesn't work out."

I began to object that I didn't think the police would guard private vehicles but Marge gave me a withering look, and I quickly jumped in the car with Julitta and Regine, and we all took off in different directions. One minute we were going to the police, the next we were going to the crash, and in this minute we were going in both directions. I was having trouble keeping up with who was where and what we were trying to do - the plan kept changing. It was getting late in the afternoon, and we still had not organized anything about dealing with our upside-down Land Rover. When we arrived at the police station, we found our truck driver had driven from his store to the police station and again offered to help us.

"Jump in," he said, "Let's go to your Landrover right now."

I got into the truck along with a couple of the police. Julitta looked exhausted from all of the stress of the day, so Regine decided it was better that they go back to Binga and wait for us. I had to keep repeating to myself where everyone was - "Marge is at the crash site with the Methodist minister, Julitta and Regine are going back to Binga, and I am riding in the truck."

The truck driver looked at me, "what?" he said.

"Oh, nothing." I couldn't believe I had just said all of that out loud.

The ride was slow because every few miles the driver stopped to pick up a hitchhiker. By the time we reached the crash site, there were 11 guys in the truck including the two policemen who had volunteered to come and me. Marge was there waiting for us with the Minister. As the two police officers got out of the back of the truck, she looked at me and smiled. Damn! Marge was right again! The driver, an older man with a short black beard, jumped out of the truck and walked over to our car.

"Oh my," he said, "I know we can get this right." He ordered us all to straighten the vehicle so that it laid parallel to the road. We pushed and heaved until we pivoted it alongside the road. "Now push it over," he ordered everyone. All 11 of us began to rock the vehicle until it rolled onto its side. "Hurry up, man, and get it on its wheels. It's leaking out all the oil," the driver shouted. We lifted the Land Rover up until it was high enough off the ground that it rolled over on its own and bounced down on all four wheels. We all cheered as the car stood upright for the first time in over 8 hours. We pulled the roof up enough so that I could sit in the driver's seat. "We're going to jump it," the driver said. He got a piece of sturdy rope from a box in the back of his truck, and a couple of the guys tied one end around the front axle of the car and the other end to the back of the truck. I depressed the clutch, put the stick into first gear and gave the thumbs-up signal to the driver. The Land Rover lurched forward as the rope tightened and we began to roll down the road. I let up on the clutch hoping the engine would catch. The vehicle dug in, and I jammed in the clutch and the brake.

"Try again," I yelled.

Same result.

"Again."

Same result. I felt discouraged, but this truck driver wouldn't give up, and on the fourth pull a great belch of black smoke blew out of the tail pipe, and the engine roared to life. I couldn't believe it. Everyone jumped and yelled and danced in the middle of the road. The guys all climbed back into the truck and Marge, and I followed close behind in the Land Rover. Marge looked relieved that the engine was running as we rolled back down the road the same way we'd come hours earlier. She kept handing me food and water from our picnic basket.

"You need something to eat," she said. As we bounced down the sandy road, the roof sank down on top of me. Marge did her best to push it back up, but eventually, I was driving with my head hunched down just peering over the top of the steering wheel. A few miles down the road we stopped at a river and refilled the radiator and the battery with water which had all leaked out. I showed the truck driver my roof situation.

"Get that thing off there and throw it in the back of the truck," he told the guys riding in the back.

They all jumped off the truck, pulled the roof off, and threw it in the back where it joined the doors and the front windshield all of which had come off in the crash. Our Land Rover looked like a convertible. Luckily my sunglasses had survived, and I wore them now to keep the wind out of my eyes.

"I'm going to Bulawayo now," the driver said, "where do you want me to drop your roof and doors?"

We told him to take the pieces of the Land Rover to Mater Dei Hospital in Bulawayo, the hospital where Marge had stayed with the Franciscan sisters when we first arrived. We would pay him when we got there. Marge and I took off for Binga. On the hour long drive to Binga, Marge kept pulling stuff out of our picnic basket to eat. I wanted to keep going to Bulawayo that night since I didn't know if the Land Rover would start again once I turned it off. But by the time we reached Binga and the doctor's house, it was dark. As soon as the doctor, Philip, and his wife Regine heard us, they rushed out of the house and invited us in where we found Julitta. Before I could say a word, someone put a cold beer in my hand. I can't remember anything ever tasting better. After that, it wasn't difficult to convince me to wait until the morning to go to Binga. Marge, Julitta, and I drove back down to T. Coffee's rental in our open car. Amazingly, everything worked - the lights, the turn signals, the horn. I backed the Land Rover up the steep hill to Tom Coffee's rental. I wanted to be facing downhill the next morning because I was certain I would have to jump start it again.

We woke up before dawn, got dressed, gathered what food we could find to replenish our picnic basket and climbed into the Land Rover. I turned the key hoping for a miracle, but nothing happened.

"Here goes nothing," I said.

I depressed the clutch, put it into first gear, and release the handbrake. The big beast began a slow roll down the hill, picking up speed as we neared the bottom. As I hit top speed, I let up on the clutch, and the engine belched into life. With a roofless, seven-hour drive ahead of us, I wanted to be most of the way to Bulawayo before the heat of the sun broiled us alive in the open car. As we drove on the dirt road from Binga to Kamitivi, the dust and sand from other cars blew around us and into our faces. We were glad to be finished with the dirt road when we reached Kamitivi. Making the descent into the gorge outside of town in this open vehicle seemed like a ride on a roller coaster. Driving along without a roof and doors gave us a whole new perspective on the landscape. With nothing blocking our view, it was pure bliss driving on the super highway to Bulawayo even though we did get stares and waves from every car that passed us. Seven hours later, we pulled into the convent grounds next to the hospital and parked. The truck with the rest of our car in it arrived minutes later. Once we parked the Land Rover at the convent, it never started again. We had to have it towed to the garage.

Chapter 9

Binga September 1984

T he Land Rover would take months to repair and rebuild. The sisters in Bulawayo were very kind and nursed us back to some semblance of normalcy. But we still needed to go to Harare to get the permits to build our homes in the compound in Binga. Once we felt recovered from the traumatic events of the past week, Marge and Julitta took off in a coach from Bulawayo to Harare to finish the process we started before the crash. I thought they would be gone a few days, but it took them over 2 weeks. I still hadn't come to terms with just how long everything took. With her bulldog determination, Marge camped out in the office of the official in charge of issuing the building permit. I spent my time in Bulawayo learning Tonga, smoking cigarettes and getting terribly bored. Eventually, and pretty much as a result of her unwavering force-of-will, Marge and Julitta returned with the necessary permits. And with that, we could begin to build our homes in Binga.

We traveled back to Binga via a big green bus (like the one I'd ridden from Mutoko to Harare, which seemed like a lifetime ago) and arrived there in mid-September. Without a vehicle, our life changed radically. Even though we lived in the lap of luxury, we now walked everywhere we wanted to go. Even getting the mail was a two-hour hike. Often a friendly truck driver would pick us up, and as we bumped along the sandy road up the steep hill into town, I stood in the back with the other riders, which gave me the opportunity to practice my Tonga. "Mwabuka," I said as I climbed into the back of the truck. The women laughed and in a friendly chorus all said, "Mwabuka" back to me. I tried to memorize some little phrase or question I could say on these rides in the truck like I'd done in Kariangwe with the children. Later I would remember the kindness of these drivers and try to pick up anyone who needed a ride.

We got used to riding the big green buses and walking everywhere else we needed to go. Our pace of life slowed down, and we got used to "Binga time." Rather than rushing around in our white Land Rover, we moved like everyone else; that is, one step at a time. In early October I stayed in Binga on my own for ten days while Julitta and Marge took a big green bus to Hwange for a retreat and conference with the sisters. I spent my time studying Tonga, and I did a lot of walking. I walked everywhere - to visit with my neighbors in their beautiful homes, to visit Peter Muleya in his home in town, to say Mass, to get the mail or to visit with the Doctor Philip from Sri Lanka and Doctor Xavier from Spain. It slowed down my pace but also made me more available to people. I loved those ten days on my own! I felt free to do what I wanted and found that I enjoyed my solitude and being able to engage the whole community, from the Tongas, to the Europeans, to the Ex-patriots. I didn't have to ask permission or explain why or what I planned to do to anyone. During that time, I discovered that one of our neighbors was a contractor and I asked him about building our homes in the compound; one for guests and me and one that Julitta and Marge would share. When Marge and Julitta returned, Marge and I walked over to his home and discussed the building project. He agreed to take on the job.

"I will work with him now to develop the plans," Marge said to Julitta and me.

After a few weeks, Marge brought the plans for us to examine. Neither of us had anything to add since the structures were simple two-bedroom cement block houses. Soon after, workers dug foundations for the footers. Whenever we went up to town for Mass or the mail, we stopped to see the progress. Materials arrived sporadically from Bulawayo which slowed the momentum, sometimes stopping all building for weeks on end. Knowing the pace of life in Zimbabwe and the slower pace of life in Binga we hoped it wouldn't take too long. Marge stayed on the builder and visited his home to keep up the pressure or to negotiate various finishes like the size of windows or a dutch door for the kitchen.

In mid-October, we received word from the mechanic that he had completed the repairs on our Land Rover. We made plans to take a big green bus to Bulawayo. Our next door neighbors discovered that we planned to go to Bulawayo to pick up the Land Rover and told us that their friends, visiting from Bulawayo, could give us a ride. Imagine our surprise when we discovered that the ride was a small four-seater airplane. The 8-hour bus trip became a 1.5-hour plane ride. For the past two months, we either walked, stood on the back of a truck, or sat in a big green bus crammed full of people. Marge decided that Julitta would stay behind in Binga since the plane had room for only two more passengers. She wanted to make sure the repairs were done to her satisfaction and wanted me to drive most of the way because she felt even more unsure of herself driving since the crash.

"You can take care of yourself for a few days, can't you?" She said.

Marge and I rode out to the airfield in Binga with the couple who owned the plane. From the air, you could see the villages, the Savannah, the rugged mountain ranges, rivers, and lakes created by dams. And rather than bumping along the corrugated roads on the ground, up here it was a smooth ride on the wind. They landed in Bulawayo and dropped us at the front door of the Franciscan Sisters' convent. What service! Marge and I picked up the Land Rover on November 1 and drove back to Binga the next day.

Chapter 10

Binga November 1984

B y November our houses had walls and a roof. It looked like we might move in sometime in December. Each one had two bedrooms, a bathroom, a kitchen, and a sitting room. A front porch extended across the front. Binga had no electricity, and we had running water for only an hour each morning and evening. We painted both houses dark green. I loved the way a huge tree arched over the top of my house and kept the front porch in the shade most of the day.

I decided that to learn the language I needed to do much more than sit in my room and memorize hundreds of Tonga words and read the Bible, the only piece of literature written in the Tonga language I could find. We arranged for the people in Kalungwizi, our most remote outstation, to fix up the little hut there where I could stay and immerse myself in the Tonga language and culture. Kalungwizi was a long, dusty 4-hour drive from Binga.

On Monday, November 12 I drove out of Binga on my own for 11 days in the bush.

"Take the Land Rover," Marge told me, "Julitta and I will be okay here on our own. If we need anything, it's a short walk to the camp store. Have fun."

On the way out of town, I stopped at the little store and bought myself some pop, cookies, and cigarettes. I opened the pop, lit a cigarette, popped a couple of cookies in my mouth and felt freer than I had in a long time. It felt great to be on an adventure, traveling out into the bush on my own. I didn't have any particular goal, other than to meet and talk to people as much as possible. The little school in Kalungwizi would be a great place to improve my Tonga.

I arrived in Kalungwizi in the late afternoon. People from the nearby villages came out to greet me - "Mwabuka's" all around. I couldn't believe how good the hut looked. The last time we visited, over two months earlier, the place looked terrible; crumbling walls and thatching full of holes. The people had patched up the walls and put repaired the thatch on the roof. It looked kind of cozy. This little hut had two rooms; a bedroom and a sitting room where people could visit. By now the temperatures had risen to well over 100 degrees, but the interior of the hut was remarkably comfortable with its grass thatch roof, hard-packed earthen floor, and the walls made of sun-hardened mud adobe.

Two Tonga high school students, Cephas and Lemonth, volunteered to be my guides for the week. Cephas was a tall, athletic young man with a ready smile. He seemed eager to lead me around from village to village and introduce me to everyone. Lemonth, the music director for the church, had a beautiful voice but walked with a cane because of his club foot. The two of them took it upon themselves to help me with my Tonga lessons, and plan each day's walk to the villages. Many old women came and talked to me as they walked past my little hut on their way to the bore hole (well) to get water. Although I found it difficult to understand them, they seemed to enjoy trying to teach me Tonga. These old women always seemed to be laughing. I wondered how they could feel so joyful when they never had enough to eat, lived in mud homes with grass thatch roofs, barely had enough clothes and never had shoes. It took a while for me to get used to seeing most of the women with their two front teeth knocked out (an old tradition) and smoking from pipes made out of large gourds. A village consisted of a series of rondavels which were like bedrooms for each member of the family who lived there. As each son and daughter married, they attached their bedroom to the family compound. For the most part, people lived outside, and the fire became the gathering place or the "living room." A network of trails wound around everyone's fields and passed through village after village. The trails often led through the middle of a village. Before passing through we stopped on the fringe, squatted down and called out a greeting. Then we asked permission to stay or to walk through. If we stopped to visit people rushed around getting everything ready before we could enter. First, they placed either a hand-carved wooden stool or a kind of bush "Lazy Boy," constructed from a couple of long branches, in a shady spot. Then all the residents of the village came out to greet us. At this point the host or hostess went around to each of us, squatted down, clapped her hands and said "Mwabuka." We clapped our hands and responded the same. No conversation began until the host or hostess completed greeting every single person. Most of the old women were smoking hookahs made from large hollowed-out gourds with a burn chamber on the upper neck and a hollow stick or straw driven through the gourd into the water filled chamber below. The women puffed and relit their hookahs continually. They were thrilled at my rudimentary Tonga and loved to correct my pronunciation or to teach me a new word. As time went on, I enjoyed this walking and talking part of the mission life the most. I loved seeing how people lived, how they tended their fields, what problems they encountered (mostly elephants and birds eating their crops or the lack of rain), and what the land looked like far away from the road.

At times the villagers invited us to stay for something to eat. The meal revolved around nsima and a relish to accompany it that often included okra which grew abundantly. Cooked okra had the consistency and appearance of pond scum, and in all the years I lived among the Tonga, I couldn't develop a taste for it. Eating involved taking a small wad of nsima, forming it into a cone or oval, impressing a little hollow in the top with your thumb and then dipping it into the relish. Everyone ate from a common bowl.

A few days after I arrived at Kalungwizi, all the youth decided to have a "Pungwe," or an all-night celebration of singing, dancing, and drumming. Even though I was only 33 at the time, I did not look forward to staying up all night. About 30 youth arrived after dark and built a fire. Then the singing and drumming and dancing began. I danced a bit but found it tough to keep up with their complicated steps and rhythms. At about two o'clock in the morning, I decided to call it a night, but the rest of the group continued into the early hours of the morning. I laid on my cot listening to the rhythmic drumming and the singing and dancing. Nestled snugly inside my mosquito netting safe from mosquitos and other night creatures, I fell asleep.

The next day, Sunday, the small group of people who came to church took up a collection and bought me a goat as an expression of their deep appreciation for my visit and to welcome me as their priest. Goats were expensive, so most people rarely ate meat of any kind. They had to dig deep to come up with the money. I thought a chicken might be more appropriate, but everyone was determined to buy me a goat. On Monday afternoon ten young people arrived at my house pulling a goat. I thanked them by saying "Twalumba" (thank you) over and over again, but inwardly I dreaded what I knew would come next. The boys laid the goat on its side, tied up its legs and slit its throat. The goat kicked and yelped and bled out right before my eyes. I never felt comfortable at the sight of blood, my own or the blood of any living being. So feeling a bit faint, I retreated to the inside of my little hut and waited. It wasn't long before some of the boys began tying up lengths of twine inside where I was sitting. And soon strips of freshly butchered goat were being carried ceremoniously into my dark space, shown to me with a flourish, and then hung on the twine. My sitting room became the curing room. They wanted the bloody strips of meat to dry slowly away from the sun. I can't describe the smell of drying meat, nor the look of bloody pieces of flesh, nor the thousands of flies that quickly swarmed on my supper. I had not anticipated this level of immersion. The unconditional generosity of these people who spent months' worth of wages so that I had meat to eat while I stayed with them touched me deeply. I soon learned to enjoy the goat as they covered it in salt and prepared it over an open fire, roasting it to a golden brown. Generosity was an important part of the Tonga culture. In every village where Cephas, Lemonth, and I stopped to visit, someone gave us something to take along. In one village a man gave us a dozen eggs which I planned to eat for breakfast for the next few days. When Cephas and I got back to my hut, I asked him to cook up some eggs for lunch. By the time I got to the cooking pot where he had squatted near the fire, he was scrambling all 12. Instead of a light lunch, we were going to have an egg feast. When I told him I meant a few eggs, he looked a little hurt and confused. I suppose when you have food you eat it.

I spoke a very childlike Tonga and understood a fraction of what anyone said to me unless they said it very slowly, repeated it often, and only spoke in the most straightforward and basic declarative sentences about topics whose vocabulary I had studied. Nonetheless, everyone seemed happy with my presence there.

Walking from village to village, I saw people preparing their fields to plant corn and millet, tilling the land with hand hoes. Everyone walked out at first light and came back home and in the shade by noon. People were tired and hungry by the time they got to their villages, but they still greeted me with a wave and a smile. Hand hoeing meant that they could only till and manage a few acres of corn. Everyone tried to grow enough food to live on until the next harvest. Corn is a dubious crop for Zimbabwe's arid climate. Rain fell sporadically. One year farmers might have a huge harvest and then the next season nothing. Helping people to achieve a subsistence level of living would be a real challenge since I knew next to nothing about farming.

The Tongas had very limited experience in agriculture and were trying to make the best of their "new" situation after being displaced from their traditional gardens next to the Zambezi River because of the Kariba Dam; built in the 1960's. Farming was not part of their heritage and would have been a challenge even for the most skilled in this climate. The area was more suited for a crop like cashews, which grew well in nearby Mozambique, but that would require a whole infrastructure of support, capital investment, and time to wait for the trees to grow.

High rocky bluffs surrounded the savannah where we lived. In the rainy season trees flourished, crops grew, and it looked like paradise. People lived close to nature as people must have lived in the iron age. The smells of cooking fires and animals filled the air. Roosters crowed early in the morning, and in the evening elephants trumpeted in the distant hill country. There were few vehicles except for the weekly big green bus or an occasional Land Rover, and life moved at its own pace paralleling the demands of the season. One evening I noticed roaring fires in each village and there seemed to be lots of excitement. I sat wondering what they were doing. It wasn't long before a troop of young people came from the village and stopped at the edge of my little clearing. "Bafada. Bafada" (Father. Father.) They were all shouting with excitement.

"Kweza," (Come here) I said.

They were carrying a basket full of something.

"Kuliya. Kuliya." (Eat) They told me.

It looked like they had a basket full of raisins. So I reached in and tried one. It was crunchy and a little salty, like a roasted soy bean but black.

"What is this?"

They answered with a word I didn't know, so I asked them to translate it into English for me.

One of the older boys said, "It's flying ants, Bafada. Delicious."

So I'd just eaten my first insect ever.

"Twalumba," I said.

And they all ran back to the fire in their village to eat more.

After my eleven days in the bush, I drove back to Binga, happy to return to our little haven of western civilization. When I walked into the door at Tom Coffee's rental, Marge and Julitta greeted me with a big hug. Marge had prepared a welcome-home feast for me that included cold beer that she and Julitta had purchased at the camp store. Marge was a fantastic cook, and after eating Nsima and relish for almost two weeks, her home cooked food tasted delicious. And as we all sat out on the back patio enjoying the meal and the beautiful view of Lake Kariba I shared stories of my stay out in the bush. Julitta and Marge were now eager to try it for themselves.

(Photo: Kalungwizi Church)

Chapter 11

Christmas in Binga 1984

T. Coffee's rental on Lake Kariba seemed more luxurious than ever now. And even though it felt good to get back to a more familiar way of life, it reminded me of the huge gap that existed between the way the Tongas lived and the way I did. While I faced the outer struggle with my environment and the work set before me, I was still dealing with the internal struggle of being a priest. Every time I had "quit" in my seminary years, someone convinced me to stay, and eventually, I had accepted priesthood as my fate and persevered. But life moved so slowly in Africa and held so little to distract me from these pervasive feelings of loneliness, that I just tried to get through each day -- "doing time," putting those troubling thoughts out of my mind for another occasion, and hoping they would go away.

A Home of Our Own

On December 17, 1984, we moved into our newly built homes. Marge and Julitta shared one house, and I lived in the other. Enjoying privacy for the first time in 10 months, I felt a tremendous sense of relief at having my space and being able to relax on my own. With the first part of our task completed, our presence in the community became more stable. We found the houses comfortable, and the shade of the huge tree kept me a few degrees cooler than everyone else.

We furnished our homes simply but with enough comforts to make them feel like home. My bedroom consisted of a single bed with mosquito netting, a wide shelf I built under the window to use as my desk, and a comfortable chair. My sitting room had a few wicker chairs and a coffee table. A gas stove stood in my kitchen alongside a kerosene refrigerator, which never worked, and a table and chairs. We placed a few comfortable chairs on the front porch. I had everything I needed.

Once we moved into our homes, it felt like our mission work was beginning. We had a permanent address. We set up a regular schedule of Mass in Binga twice a month and then once a month each in Nakangala and Kalungwizi. Every three weeks or so we drove to Hwange for supplies and every two months we made the trek to Bulawayo for a big shopping trip. But there was never a rush or hurry to get things done, and I missed being busy. With so much time on my hands, the questions about my life's direction rose like demons.

Our first Christmas in Binga turned out to be fun. On Christmas Eve we celebrated Mass at Kalungwizi in the early evening and then drove to Nakangala for a candlelight Mass. Our little thatch-and-mud church with half walls and the smell of goats all around made the whole scene feel like the first Christmas in Bethlehem. On the way back to Binga that night it began to rain, and the roads turned white and slippery and dangerous – almost like snow. So I put the Landrover in 4-wheel drive, slowed to 30 kph, and Marge, Julitta, and I sang carols for 2 hours while we drove back home. It was still raining when we arrived in Binga, and we stayed up late singing more hymns and toasting Christmas with glasses of brandy. After Christmas Mass in Binga the next day, a few of the men who stayed in town stopped by for tea, bread, and jam (their traditional Christmas breakfast).

Later that day we drove to Kariangwe to surprise the missionaries there, but to our surprise, they were all expecting us. Manolo had prepared a big turkey dinner, and we sang carols in Spanish, Shona, and English.

In mid-January 1985, the other Fr. Mike, from the discernment process, and Bishop Hoffman arrived in Zimbabwe for a visit. Marge insisted on meeting them in Harare by herself so she could talk to them about the mission.

"I need to have some time alone with Mike and the Bishop," she said. "I want to report to them what we have done and how the team is shaping up."

"You two can enjoy a few days with the sisters in Hwange and then pick us up in Victoria Falls."

It felt strange not to be part of the welcoming party in Harare since I knew Mike well and I had lived in the Bishop's house for the three years before I left for Zimbabwe. Julitta and I took Marge to the airport where she caught a plane to meet Mike and the Bishop, then we continued to Hwange to stay with the sisters and wait. Within a few days Marge, Mike, and the Bishop flew from Harare to Victoria Falls where Julitta and I met them with our Landrover. We visited the Falls and drank a beer at the famous Victoria Falls Hotel. Hoffman got us all talking and laughing and soon enough it was time to go. We made the long drive out to Binga. Mike and the bishop loved the gorge at Kamitivi which I now took at a faster speed. Outside of Kamitivi, I hydroplaned over the corrugated sandy roads until we reached Binga. We arrived there just before dark and showed them our new houses.

The next day we took the Bishop and Mike to Nakangala and Kalungwizi where the people welcomed them as if they were Heads of State, and then on Sunday, we celebrated a big Mass in Binga with another large crowd. Mike and the Bishop were thrilled to experience firsthand what they had only read about in our letters. We were surprised at how much we accomplished in the past twelve months. We'd bought a Land Rover in South Africa and driven it to Binga. I'd learned the language well enough to be able to say Mass and preach in Tonga. We'd built two houses and were now living in them. We'd taken over three outstations and were preparing to start more. We'd survived the Landrover crash and had the car back again. Marge's "force of will" made things happen.

On Sunday afternoon the Bishop and I took a walk on our own. It was the first time we were alone since they arrived. After we had walked for a few minutes, he stopped and said,

"Shane (his nickname for me), you are fantastic!"

He applauded my rapport with the people, their genuine positive regard for me, my command of the language and my preaching. I thanked him and then began to pour out my heart to him about how difficult I found working in the remoteness of Binga. He listened to me and encouraged me to talk it out with Marge.

"Let her know how you feel. Give it some more time and see what happens," the Bishop told me.

It felt good to share these struggles and frustrations with someone. But I wasn't ready to talk about it yet, maybe in the same way I had avoided facing my regrets about becoming a priest. Avoidance seemed easier than confrontation, but it took a terrible toll on me.

We spent a few days at the Hwange Game Park and then a day at Victoria Falls. On the last evening, we enjoyed the sunset cruise on the Zambezi River. That was when many of the animals came to the river to drink. The boat floated along the shore while we sipped cocktails and enjoyed the beauty of Africa in marvelous comfort. The boat came close enough to the Falls for us to see and feel the spray, and then it turned back to the dock. The next day we said our farewells at the airport and Mike and the Bishop flew home. Funny, but in all of our conversations alone and together, I never discovered why Marge had wanted to meet them alone or what she told them.

After they had left, life settled back into a routine. One bright spot was that since the crash, our friendship with the Sri Lankan doctor Philip and his German wife Regine had grown and deepened. Marge, Julitta, and I often went for a meal or to spend an evening with them, and sometimes I dropped in for a chat. Philip and Regine ran the Binga Hospital which was always full of patients. That first year in Binga I came down with some internal problem that caused terrible diarrhea. I couldn't be too far from the bathroom. Philip and Regine had invited us for lunch, but I couldn't go because of diarrhea. Philip walked over to the house and came right up to the window of my bedroom next to my bed. He took one look at me and said,

"You are dehydrated, man. If you don't start drinking something right now, I am going to put you in the hospital on a drip."

As much as I appreciated the availability of the hospital in Binga, it was not a place I wanted to go. I began to force fluids. I had to report my progress to Philip regularly via Marge and Julitta who hovered over me like two geese with a fallen gosling.

Marge checked on my fluid intake regularly. "Mike, you have to keep drinking."

I could hear the concern in her voice.

"I've had friends who died in my last mission because of this. You've got to keep drinking."

I kept drinking water, all the while thinking it was too bad it couldn't be something stronger!

Chapter 12

Our First New Station March 1985

On our visits to Nakangala and Kalungwizi, we spent most of our time walking from village to village visiting or praying for the sick. We never knew what to expect. As time went on people often brought someone who was ill or experiencing some difficulty and asked us to pray for them. Lemonth reported that people often got better. Our reputation was spreading.

On one outing we were walking through a forest and stopped in a village where the people invited us to stay for supper. The people provided Marge, Julitta, and myself with large carved stools where we sat in a place of honor in the center of the village. Each member of the village came up and greeted us very formally and then went back to cooking nsima. After half an hour the women placed a bowl of nsima in front of us as well as six little-roasted birds, the size of robins. They looked like small turkeys. The head of the village showed me how to pop the little-roasted birds into my mouth crunching the whole thing, bones and all. They watched as I picked up one of the little birds, examined it carefully heightening the suspense and then popped it in my mouth. The whole village watched and waited as I crunched and swallowed.

I looked around and said the only word I could think of, "Kulweela," elongating the double "ee" as in "Kulweeeeela."

I was trying to think of the word for "delicious, " and only the word "sweet" came to mind. But everyone got the idea that I liked it and laughed at my wrong use of the word and clapped and the bacembele (old women) ululated (that high-pitched yodel). I asked how they caught the birds and the headman told me he laid a sticky trap line in the woods baited with seed and when the birds came to eat they got stuck in a sticky, goopy mixture made from tree sap. Then he arrived and collected the catch.

The Tongas believed that every person had a spirit connection with something in nature. They never ate an animal with which they felt a connection. With my new Tonga name, Syamuunda, "the one who cares for the field," I decided my spirit connection was with mice. Whenever people served mice - and mice showed up frequently on the menu - I could politely decline.

In March, Marge announced, "We need to start expanding our outstations. We can't just keep visiting the same places over and over again."

I was beginning to feel comfortable with our routine visits out to Nakangala and Kalungwizi but had to agree that there was a lot more we could be doing. The Tongas lived in village settlements governed by a Chief. The government built schools in the midst of a Chief's area, and the school became a central point for activity. Marge devised a plan to visit schools in each zone where we wanted to start a new outstation and make the school our central point for meeting with people.

Instead of leaving Binga on Friday morning for Nakangala or Kalungwizi, Marge decided we would go on Thursday and spend the day visiting one or two schools. Many of the schools were placed deep in the bush down long, rutted tracks. We had seen the sign for a school down one of these tracks on our visits out to Nakangala and decided that would be a good place to test out the plan. We turned off the road and picked our way along a narrow track that wound through the overgrowth of bush for miles. After half an hour we pulled into a clearing with a small school. The headmaster, hearing our Landrover approaching stood in the middle of the school grounds and came up to us as we got out of the vehicle.

"Good afternoon," he said in perfect English.

He was a Shona teacher who had found a job teaching in this remote area. He invited us into one of the small classrooms and sat down. Then Marge described our plan to start a small mission outstation in the area, and she asked him to get the children to invite their parents to meet us when we returned in a week. The headmaster agreed and then we picked our way back down the track and then drove on to Nakangala.

The next week we arrived as promised. The headmaster showed us a classroom where we could spend the night and another that we could use for our service. We weren't sure when anyone would arrive since there were no clocks, and schedules were loose and flowed with the demands of life, so we unpacked and waited under a large fig tree that grew a few hundred feet from the school and in full view of the villages.

"We'll let everyone see we're here," Marge said, "then they'll know we aren't leaving."

We waited for hours. As the sun was setting the first few brave villagers approached us and greeted us and then sat on the edge of the clearing, waiting to see what would happen next. Slowly more and more people began to arrive. Eventually, enough people were there that we all walked to the classroom. I lit our kerosene lamps. Everyone sat in the small student desks or on the floor, waiting for us to do something. Showtime! I stood up in front of my little congregation and in my best bad Tonga explained why we were there. I read a short passage from the Tonga Bible and then preached a little sermon about God's love for them. Then I taught them a song in Tonga. Everyone joined in but it sounded a little weak without the drum accompaniment I was used to in the other two more developed outstations. The whole thing lasted about an hour. By the time we finished everyone was excited by our visit and on the way out asked us when we would come back again. After all, it wasn't every day that a big white guy came to their village to teach them new songs in their language. We promised to return again in two weeks.

We used this same simple method in other places and slowly began to expand the number of villages we would visit. At first, we slept in the school buildings, but that meant sleeping in buildings with no doors, exposed to whatever wildlife roamed the area at night and getting out of the building before school started in the morning. Marge thought that if we pitched tents near the school, it would be easier and safer for us to stay out in the bush. We asked friends and family at home to send us small backpacking tents. We liked the idea of sleeping in tents where we at least felt safe from animals and snakes and could be dry if it rained. Within a month three small tents and sleeping bags arrived by mail. Camping became a fun way for us to get out and see the natural beauty of our territory. Our favorite camping spot was under the huge fig tree we'd sat under on that first visit. The tree towered 75 feet in the air with branches that spread out in such a wide arc that we could pitch all of our tents under its shade and still have plenty of room. From that vantage point, we could see the forest behind us, the villages right in front of us and in the far off distance, the mountains rising. Each time we pulled into the school clearing, the word spread that the "mukuwa" (Europeans or Whites) had arrived and after people finished their evening nsima and put their goats away, they walked to our campsite.

Within a few months, we visited another village called Malube, not far from Binga. When we arrived, we found about 70 people all dancing and singing. The headmaster of the school had told people of our intention to come and visit, and the whole village came out to greet us. The Headman of the village, the Chief's second in command, told me that many years before a missionary came to visit but then never returned. They were determined to make us feel so welcome that we would come back. They succeeded! After I had finished my simple little message about the light of God's love for them, I asked if anyone had any questions. The Headman voiced their biggest concern: "We want someone right here in our village who can lead us out of darkness." They asked us to leave a Bible with them so they could read it for themselves.

Marge's expansion idea was working. Sometimes we returned two or three times before we got what we considered to be a crowd - about 20 people. Over time we established 15 new little communities by going out and sitting under a tree until people came to see us. In all that time we never coaxed people with gifts of food or clothing, but we always gave people a lift to the road or Binga. I remembered how good the truck drivers had been to me during those months when I was without any vehicle. Someone always needed to go to Binga, so we became a bush taxi service. It was something tangible that people needed, and they began to see us as helpful and involved with them in this simple way. The fact that I made an effort to speak Tonga also made a huge impression.

(Photo: The sisters' house in Binga – Mike and me)

Chapter 13

New Friends July / September 1985

Binga attracted many international aid workers. By 1985, an American family, a Danish family, and a Dutch worker had moved into our compound. Now I had some other "mukuwa" with whom I shared a common purpose - to help bring people out of poverty and into basic subsistence living.

The Americans came from Colorado and worked in an agricultural center in Binga; teaching the Tonga good practices in animal husbandry and farming. The Danes did similar work with the Tongas out in their villages and fields. Both families built their houses in our compound about ten months after we moved to Binga and I found myself walking over to visit them more and more frequently. I loved going to their homes to listen to music or to have a chat. Terry, the other American, and I started to play cribbage on Sunday evenings, usually with a couple of shots of bourbon to help the game along. I enjoyed having some male companionship.

One evening all of the women decided to have a "girls' night out" at the safari camp down near the lake. They pre-ordered an excellent meal and took off for the evening. I decided to read a novel and drink a few beers on my own. As I sat in the shade under my big tree, I heard someone crashing through the bush behind my house. Terry, the American, emerged from the bush and stood over me.

"Mike, Peter (the Dane) and I are going to have a man's night out too. Come on over; we're going to fry up some steaks and drink some beer," he said.

That sounded great! The beer flowed, the steaks tasted delicious, and I laughed until I cried.

I visited Philip and Regine often as well. Regine was in charge of finding blood donors for the hospital, and the guys who frequented the local beer joint in Binga were her frequent victims. One Sunday she was desperate for blood and drove from the hospital to the school just as I finished Mass.

"Mike, we need your blood right now. Get in the ambulance," She said.

I got in the ambulance along with a couple of other guys from the congregation, and she whisked us off to the hospital. As my blood began to flow, I realized that I hadn't eaten anything that morning. The room was hot. My head began to spin. The next thing I knew, Dr. Philip and Dr. Xavier were hauling me out on a stretcher and into the surgical recovery room. Someone always needed blood at the hospital, and I was willing to donate, but the hospital staff developed a unique protocol for me after that incident. Sometimes Regine sent a hospital van to pick me up because we had no phone. She set up a special room for me complete with a bed. As I laid down, someone gave me a little something to eat. Once I looked calm, one staff distracted me on the side opposite while a nurse inserted the needle for the blood draw. Then Regine assigned someone else to watch me during the procedure. When a nurse withdrew the needle, a staff member brought more food. I could only leave when Philip gave the thumbs up. That protocol prevented any further fainting incidents.

That evening Regine invited me to have dinner with them, to thank me for my blood and to make sure I was recovering from the trauma of that morning's blood draw. During dinner an argument broke out between Regine and Philip about their newborn daughter Naomi. Naomi was born with a rectal prolapse, a condition where the rectum loses internal support and slips outside the body. Regine and Naomi went a few weeks earlier to a hospital in Bulawayo for the surgery to correct this. At the time I had no idea about any of it and so was completely taken by surprise when on the way back from Hwange on a shopping trip I found Philip standing at the crossroads hitchhiking to Bulawayo. I stopped and asked Philip what he was doing out there on the road in the middle of nowhere.

"I'm trying to get to Bulawayo before the bloody surgeon starts the procedure on Naomi to make sure he isn't drunk."

"Hop in," I told him, "Let's go to Bulawayo."

We stopped for the night at a mission on the way and early the next morning took off for the hospital in Bulawayo. Philip made it in time for the surgery and all went well. As that whole episode was being retold at dinner, Philip accused Regine of having the defective genes which she passed on to Naomi. Regine flatly denied it and accused Philip of covering up his own defective genes. Philip told her she was an uptight, anal German. She said he was a loose Sri Lankan. The argument was heating up when I broke in.

"Philip, I am one hundred percent sure that Naomi's condition could not have come from your DNA. I know this without a doubt."

He said, "You have no medical training. How could you possibly know this?"

"Because, Philip, you are a perfect ass hole."

There was just the briefest pause, a look of utter disbelief that I, a catholic priest, had said those words. And then the whole gathering erupted in sustained laughter.

These families became close friends and helped anchor me. They also challenged me when they saw my underlying unhappiness, despite my best efforts to put on a "happy face." It wasn't that they didn't think I believed in the work, it was more that they didn't believe I loved the work. Later, a doctor in Bulawayo challenged me in the same way as I lay in the hospital with my third bout of malaria.

"You don't love what you are doing at all," he said, "you are flat."

I knew he was right, but I had no idea of what to do about any of this. I had known this even before my ordination day. I didn't love being a priest. I struggled with the isolation of our life in Binga. For the time being, I decided to hang in there and hope that something might happen to change a trajectory toward despair that seemed inevitable. I would have never guessed in a million years how dramatically that path would change. But in the meantime, I hunkered down.

My Inner Struggles, Visitors, and Cold Beer

Visitors from the USA continued to come to see us. Marge, Julitta, and I developed a plan that included a short stay in Harare and Bulawayo, a 5 – 7-day tour of our outstations, and then 3 – 5-day visit to the Game Park at Hwange finishing at Victoria Falls. The last night always included the sunset cruise on the Zambezi River.

In July 1985, my friends Fr. Bernie and Sr. Nancy from Toledo came and stayed with us for two weeks. As usual, we enjoyed a few days in Bulawayo and Harare. No one could believe the extent of the amenities that these cities offered. The luxuries in the city stood in stark contrast to the Bush experience of Binga. Bernie and Nancy loved it and spent a night out in our mud huts in Nakangala. Their ministry in Toledo centered around the African American community, so they couldn't wait to come to Africa. As usual, the Tonga people welcomed Bernie and Nancy and gave them a chicken and other gifts. I took the opportunity to talk to them both about my struggles and the isolation I felt in Binga. Bernie was so upset about my situation that he refused to shave until I came home.

In September 1985 my Mom, Dad, and brother Fred came for two weeks. Even in their late 60's, Mom and Dad were quite adventurous.

In 1982 I took them on a trip to Germany, where we discovered my Grandfather's home in Wallersdorf, Bavaria, and ate in a Bierstube where my Grandfather had eaten decades earlier. But Africa was an entirely different kind of adventure. The Tongas revered elders and considered this visit a great honor. During their stay, Mom, Dad, Fred and I laughed and reminisced and drank a lot of beer. Marge, Julitta and I took them on the usual city tour and then out to the bush. Marge loved to cook and made many of her favorite recipes for them. Dad loved it. The second week I spent with them on my own. We rented a beautiful cabin right on the Zambezi. It all felt exotic, with warthogs on the path and monkeys with bright blue testicles in the trees. One evening we had drinks and dinner at the Victoria Falls Hotel, which after two years in the country had become a regular stopping place for me. Sitting in the dining room with linens and crystal on the table, waiters in white jackets, overhead fans, and beautiful flowers everywhere, it was hard to imagine that a few miles away people lived in abject poverty.

When I had the chance to be alone with my closest and dearest friends and my family they discovered my "double life." On the outside I performed magnificently, achieving great things, but on the inside, I felt lonely and unfulfilled. The long days in the parish with so much scheduled helped me avoid what I now faced in those moments when I was alone and without any diversion. It was clear to them (and to me) that I was not happy. But I still had not decided what to do about it. Somewhere along the line, a thought got stuck in my head that God's will for me was to lead a life of deprivation, suffering for the greater good. Happiness was for others, not for me. Who planted this seed in my subconscious? Where did I learn this idea of a slow and tortured martyrdom rather than the pursuit of happiness? I don't know where it began, but it held fast. I just did my time.

Chapter 14

Outstations Continue to Grow October 1985

Through the Spring and Summer, we concentrated our efforts on visiting schools between our mission in Binga and Nakangala, and by October we had established eleven new places which we began to visit regularly. As a result of our visits at schools deep in the bush, word began to travel, and more villagers asked us to come and visit them. Now we no longer used the headmasters to connect; people came to see us on their own. The farthest place we visited was about 6 hours away and close to Lake Kariba, called Chuunga. Upon our first visit there we found a completely equipped tourist village. It consisted of round cottages, each topped with thick grass thatch. The compound had a central kitchen/dining room, and a large swimming pool. After driving through the bush on terrible roads for hours, we were in the most remote part of our remote section of the country, so it was a surprise to find such pleasant/well-appointed accommodation. The Bush was always full of surprises. The European couple who ran this hunters' camp and everyone else took a plane or a boat to get there. They told us we were welcome to stay with them when they weren't busy with hunters.

Thursday to Sunday we stayed at our outstations. Monday and Tuesday we relaxed a bit in Binga and took care of housekeeping and gardening. There was always something to fix or a shelf that needed to be built and so to keep myself occupied I became the handyman and gardener for the team. I also spent the time working on my next sermons, tediously writing them out in English and then translating them word-for-word into Tonga. I longed for the day when I could write what I wanted to say in Tonga without going through this process of writing and translating. Wednesday was "pack up" day when we filled the Land Rover with all the supplies for the next four days of living in the bush; that is, our tents, sleeping gear, clothing, food, and cooking supplies. We tried to spread out our meeting places so that people could walk a reasonable distance, a few miles, to get to one of our Masses.

We carried with us first aid supplies to treat wounds. We took people to the hospital frequently when we went back to Binga. Many of the wounds were serious. In one case I helped a man with leprosy whose wounds were full of maggots. Dr. Philip gave us a supply of bandages and antiseptic ointments.

"Philip, I don't have any medical training at all. What if I do the wrong thing? I'm a priest, not a doctor," I said.

"You're a human being with some compassion aren't you? Get over it, man!"

He ordered me to wear surgical gloves whenever I treated anyone. We filled many different functions, everything from entertainment, to spiritual healing, to taxi service, to first aid. One day a family came and squatted on the edge of our camp. A young girl had burned her leg badly. The family had covered the wound with a raw egg which had congealed over the burned area. The injury looked well-protected. I cleaned it, put on some burn salve and dressing, and then showed the family how to change the bandages. Julitta, Marge and I took turns with the big tin medical box. Someone would come to the edge of our camp and squat down as was customary. If someone needed medical attention, one of us got up and attended to them. Our best times as a team was on these weekly trips out to the bush. Marge and Julitta visited with the women and children while I talked to the men. The women welcomed Julitta and Marge and felt more comfortable with them. My "whiteness" and my size made me a little intimidating since I towered over most of the men.

A few times children would catch sight of me and run screaming, "Momma, it's a ghost!"

My Tonga language skills improved so that I managed longer conversations without constantly having to look up words or ask the children to translate for me. I loved public speaking. In college, I took every speech class I could. And I loved being a high school teacher in Toledo and Tiffin. I decided to create some longer talks about topics of spirituality or practical things anyone could do, like visiting and praying for the sick. Later these little gatherings would turn into two-day conferences where we explored topics like farming or fishing. Once a month, we invited everyone from the area to come to a particular station and spend the whole day with us. We provided food – nsima and a goat – and then spent the day together talking. At first, I used poster paper to write some of the key points I wanted to make in Tonga. But I noticed that even though people could understand my Tonga, none of the older people could read and so the children had to explain what I had written. I realized two things: 1) I had to become simpler and more concrete, and 2) I was disrespecting the elders, especially the "bacembele," (old women) who held a place of honor in the community. When I wrote words on the poster paper, they depended on the children to translate what I wrote for them. I devised a plan that involved stick figures.

First I outlined my teaching in English, and then wrote it down word for word in Tonga, simplifying my talk. Then I pre-drew the illustrations for my teaching lightly in pencil on the poster paper so that in the middle of the talk I could just draw over the lines. I liked the effect of drawing the illustrations in the midst of the talk because it gave people a little relief from listening to me and made a more dramatic point as the picture slowly emerged.

People watched as I drew my illustrations, and had great fun guessing what picture was emerging as I drew. A few of the bacembele were sitting right up in front now as I spoke and drew on the poster paper.

Then one of the bacembele started to laugh, "Look everyone! Bafada has already drawn the picture. I can see it. I can see it."

Everyone strained to see my pre-drawn pencil drawings on the poster paper and the whole group, including me, started to laugh.

"All right. All right." I said. "Now you know my little trick. Wait to see how it turns out."

That was a turning point, and instead of being the big white guy know-it-all, by being able to laugh at myself and join in the fun, I became less frightening, more friendly, and just like them. The illustrations were crude, but they captured the essence of the teaching so that the bacembele could easily remember everything I said. At the end of one long afternoon focused on visiting and praying for the sick, I asked for some volunteers to explain and act out the entire day's lesson. Immediately two bacembele jumped up and came to the front of the little church-hut. Without using the illustration in any way, they acted it out perfectly. Everyone clapped and laughed and ululated at their success. From that moment on, I became the stick-figure illustrator, and I never wrote another word on a piece of poster paper again.

Teaching helped me to feel connected to the people. For the first time since I had arrived more than 18 months earlier, I felt the focus of my attention moving outward. I loved this new way of teaching, and I looked forward to these sessions as much as the villagers did. We broke up the day with singing and dancing. Everyone jumped to their feet at the first hint of a song. These people were the poorest of the poor even by Zimbabwean standards, yet they possessed an incredible resilience and exuberance for life.

Occasionally I traveled out to the bush on my own, leaving Marge and Julitta in Binga. At night the stars shone so brightly I could see to walk, and the full moon cast so much light that I could read. There I experienced a closeness to the Divine Presence if only briefly, something deeper, more primal and ancient. I began to sense that the deep spirituality I sought was not contingent upon being a priest but rather in letting go and becoming connected with nature and with others. These Tongas reached out to me as much as the stars and the moon in this night sky. I had thought to be a priest was the only way of being close to God, but in those moments I felt closer to God than I had ever been in church.

Many more people came to visit us in Binga; the local Tongas, our new expatriate friends, and people from America. So we built a gazebo under the big tree right next to my house to make them feel welcome. It had a concrete floor, a short rock wall enclosing the gazebo, and a thick grass thatch roof. We felt comfortable meeting anyone there. It was cool and often breezy, and except for the occasional snake, it felt safe and secure. We even slept out there with mosquito nets if our bedrooms were full of visitors.

By the end of 1985, I had been in Zimbabwe for almost two years. I was experiencing stunning connections with the local people despite the demons of my loneliness that still reared their heads in those times of solitude. But that was all about to change.

Chapter 15

Mary Arrives November 1985

In November 1985 Marge, Julitta, and I went to Bulawayo for one of our regular shopping trips. We left after Sunday Mass in Binga and arrived in the early evening at the Franciscan Convent in Bulawayo. We never got over the fact that in the morning we were in the most remote area of the country with no electricity and limited running water, and by the afternoon we were in a city that looked like any other bustling European metropolis. The sisters always seemed glad to see us.

The next day we shopped at a large warehouse store that had an amazing array of food and other supplies. The shelves were stacked from floor to ceiling with boxes of food and other items we could never find in Hwange. In Binga, we rested on Monday, but in Bulawayo, we couldn't wait until the store opened. Whatever we bought had to fit into the Land Rover for the 6-hour trip back to Binga.

Later that morning I was cutting hair for two of the sisters. I had disclosed on one trip that I had learned how to cut hair while I was a student in Rome. From that point on, these two sisters choose me as their new coiffeur.

"Michael, I think I'm going to need a trim while you're here," one said.

"I'll need one as well," the other said.

"Tomorrow, after shopping, we'll get you both looking right."

They both smiled and disappeared into the convent. I knew enough about scissor-cutting and layering to be dangerous, but the sisters seemed happy enough with the outcome. The veil they still wore covered any mistakes I made with my scissors. But they appeared to enjoy the chit chat as much as the haircut. I talked about my family at home or the latest round of visitors who had come to visit us in Binga, and they told me about their families in England and Ireland. Sometimes we commiserated on the "team problems" I experienced, or they would share something about their "nun" problems.

"What we say in the barbershop, stays in the barbershop," I said.

I enjoyed doing this little act of kindness for these two as well as saying Mass for the whole community of sisters while I stayed there. All of the sisters went out of their way to make me feel like a part of their family.

I took a long nap that day and got up a little later than usual. Sr. Jacinta ruled the kitchen, and when tea time rolled around in the afternoon, you never knew what might be there. She loaded the pastry cart with cakes, cookies, little muffins, and more. This day I missed the treats, so I settled for a cup of tea and sat down. A new, younger sister sat on the other end of the table on her own. She had dark hair with a few streaks of gray and a beautiful oval face with hazel eyes.

When she saw me sitting down, she looked up and said, "Hello. I'm Mary."

"Your voice doesn't sound English or Irish to me," I told her.

"It better not be. I'm Australian."

"Glad to meet you. I'm Mike."

Her face lit up, "Mike from Binga?"

"Yes indeed." I thanked my lucky stars that I had slept a little later, and now had this young sister's attention all to myself.

"Oh! I hoped I would get to meet you," she said, "I read about you in an article in Review for Religious that your friend Fr. Peter wrote. You sounded interesting, and I wasn't sure whether I'd bump into you. Now here you are."

I wrote to Pete regularly but had no idea he quoted one of my letters in an article. I felt grateful to Pete that he had unwittingly broken the ice for me with this lovely young sister. We sat and drank tea and talked for over an hour. Finally, I thought, someone my age to talk to now. And if she was stationed here in Bulawayo, I could get to see her every time we came for shopping. She had just arrived in Zimbabwe the previous day. Before coming to Zimbabwe, she had lived in Rome for a year, and that kicked off a whole conversation about places we both knew there.

"We lived outside of the city center, so we had to take a bus into town. I loved all the pasta dishes we got to eat. Some of the other sisters complained about the lack of potatoes and the terrible tea. But I loved trying all the new foods," she said.

I liked her spunk. We talked about food and places in Rome we'd visited. She told me about going to the "station churches" in Rome during Lent. These were churches that only opened once a year on a particular day in Lent. When I told her that I was part of the small group of guys from my college in Rome who'd begun that practice in 1976 she couldn't believe it.

"There are at least a hundred people who go now," she said.

"There were only five of us who did it back then," I said. I could tell Mary was impressed by that. She loved England and Rome but wasn't sure about coming to Africa. I told her it would take some time to adjust. "Be patient."

Over the course of the week in Bulawayo, I got to know more about this new sister. We seemed to be bumping into one another a lot. Sometimes I would sit with her at tea time and sometimes we would sit in the courtyard in the evening and talk. Her whole face would light up when she saw me, and we'd stop and chat for a moment and then she'd run off to wherever she was going. She never walked slowly and when I did have time to walk with her it was all I could do to keep up even though I was six inches taller.

"Hurry up, slow poke," she'd say when I began to fall behind. And then she'd laugh.

I enjoyed all of the other sisters, but I looked forward to the times when Mary and I had a chance to talk alone. Conversation flowed between us, and it would get quite late and dark before we knew it. We had so much in common! Our birthdays were only a few months apart. We both spent time in Rome. She went to physiotherapy school at St. Thomas and had lived in London, and I had lived in Liverpool. She left home for the convent at age 19, while I was 17 when I went to college seminary. She was the firstborn of 13, and I was the firstborn of 4. It seemed that we had endless shared experiences and there didn't appear to be enough time to talk about them all. Now besides looking forward to the warehouse store to shop in each time we came to Bulawayo I looked forward to seeing Mary. In the midst of this dark cloud I'd been living in, a spark of light broke through, and her name was Mary Daniel. This visit to Bulawayo ended too quickly and by Thursday Marge, Julitta, and I drove back to Binga where we got into the schedule of Masses and visits to outstations.

That year the rains came in December which made travel on the roads almost impossible. The rainy season was so different from the weather in the rest of the year. Days before the rains came the heat and humidity began to build to an almost intolerable level. Binga had a hot, dry climate. When the rains finally came, they brought with them an incredible relief. This desert-like landscape blossomed back to life in a few days. It sometimes rained for days or weeks. The air was fresh but so damp that everything felt wet all the time. Like a big snow in Ohio, during the rains, we hunkered down until the storms stopped and the roads dried out.

In January 1986, two years after I arrived in Zimbabwe, Bishop Hoffman came back for a vacation with Fr. Armstrong. He told me that he wanted to have time off with me in Zimbabwe – no sisters. The Bishop had to be more formal when around the sisters. He might also have been worried about my state of mind and wanted to come and see how I was doing. The two of us had bonded during the years I lived at the Cathedral, and he seemed more like my uncle than my superior. I met them at the airport in Harare. After a night in the city, part of the usual tour, I decided to show them the whole eastern part of the country beginning at the resort area around the dam at Lake Kariba. We took off on the highway for Kariba, about 5 hours north of Harare. The ride from Harare to Kariba took us through flat terrain under cultivation. There were huge mega farms as well as small holdings. It felt great to be driving along the highway without a care in the world for the next two weeks. Armstrong was the priest who took care of all the priests considered "strays" by the Bishop. He was funny, cynical, and spiritual but in an unconventional way. Hoffman was more straightforward but never missed an opportunity to get a "dig" in if he found an opening. I felt like "fresh meat" for these guys, and we laughed ourselves sick all the way to Kariba. I could feel my tension draining away. We stayed at a beautiful resort at the far eastern end of the lake near the Lake Kariba Dam. Hoffman and Armstrong needed a couple of days to sleep off their jet lag, and so we walked around the grounds, laid in the sun, read novels, and tried different tropical drink concoctions at the local pub to determine which drink had the most appeal. Besides reading books, this mixological research took up a good deal of our time.

"Shane, try this one," the bishop said as he would hand me another umbrella-topped drink.

We decided tropical drinks were the best medicine to help them both get over the jet lag and become acclimated to the summer heat.

After two nights we headed to the Eastern Highlands of Zimbabwe. The ride to the Eastern Highlands took us up into a mountainous region of Zimbabwe covered in pine trees. People called it "Little Switzerland." The climate and the landscape were different than that in Binga with its dry savannah and rocky bluffs. The drive took almost 8 hours, but in the end, we came to a small cottage on a lake in the midst of a thick pine forest. Armstrong pulled a chair out into the sun and pretty much camped there sunning himself and reading novels for the next three days. Hoffman and I took long walks into the forest, read books, and enjoyed the peace and quiet of the place. During that time, I shared with him my struggles with the priesthood and my loneliness. I told him about meeting Mary and how much I liked her. He listened and suggested again that I talk to Marge about my difficulties. He enjoyed hearing about Mary and told me he wanted to meet her. He knew I enjoyed female companionship and he thought having a friend here would help relieve the loneliness. But my feelings for Mary were evolving quickly from friendship into something deeper. He wanted to hear more about Mary, and I loved talking about her. As much as I enjoyed being with these guys, I kept thinking about Mary and how much I would like to show her all of these sites and experience them with her. My conversation with Hoffman lasted so long that after two hours Armstrong burst into the cabin.

"Are you guys gonna come up for air?" He said. "I was afraid to come in. But I can't hold it any longer." And he rushed into the bathroom.

After a few days Armstrong, Hoffman and I moved to a golfing resort. Armstrong and I decided to try to create the perfect Bloody Mary while Hoffman took a walk out on the golf course. We would each order a Bloody Mary and then carefully count the drops of Tabasco and Worcestershire Sauce that we thought made the perfect drink. Not satisfied with the result we would order another round altering the formula slightly. An hour or so later Hoffman was astonished to find us still tweaking Bloody Marys. Both Armstrong and I felt that we were on the verge of some significant discovery, but it was unclear at that point what it was we were trying to discover. A few days later we left the Eastern Highlands and stopped at the convent in Bulawayo for a night. The sisters put on a big cookout in the courtyard for the Bishop, Armstrong and me. I kept looking around trying to find Mary, but there was such a crush of sisters crowded into the courtyard all eager to meet Hoffman that I keep getting distracted. I was starting to worry that she wouldn't show when I saw her rushing into the party looking flushed. When she caught my eye, she smiled and walked over to where I stood with the Bishop.

"Jim, this is Mary. Mary this is my Bishop."

"I've heard a lot about you from Mike," he said, "very glad to finally meet you."

The three of us sat together as Sister Jacinta served up the "American hamburgers" she had been grilling.

"Mike told me you spent a year in Rome, Mary," the Bishop said.

That launched us into a whole conversation about food, museums, and Italian buses. Halfway through dessert, Mary looked at her watch.

"Oh my God. I've got to get to my Ndebele lesson," she said. And She jumped up and ran out of the courtyard, skirts flying. The Bishop was laughing at her abrupt exit.

"I like her, Shane," he said.

Me too!

I didn't get to spend much time with Mary that trip, although we did get to talk one evening where I finally had the chance to give her the present I'd bought for her.

She slowly unwrapped it. "It's ginger beer," she said. "You remembered."

When I met Mary in November, she had told me how much she enjoyed ginger beer. Attached to the bottle was a note where I'd written, "I am so glad you are here." She seemed touched by the gesture and my sentiment but didn't show it. Years later she told me that she had danced around her room hugging the bottle and rereading that little note. The next evening Mary and I talked late sitting in the chairs around the courtyard. Everyone else had gone to bed. When I got up to go back to my room, Mary put her arms around me and kissed me, just a peck on the lips.

The next morning, Hoffman, Armstrong, and I stopped at the game park in Hwange, where we spent two days looking for animals and then ended the trip in Victoria Falls. Marge and Julitta met us there, and on the last night, we took the sunset cruise on the Zambezi. We saw them off at the airport the next day and then drove back to Binga and reality.

Chapter 16

Mike and Jules February 1986

On February 6, 1986, the other Fr. Mike and a lay missionary, Julie Wright, joined our team. It was great to see Mike again and to meet Julie, whom I called "Jules." Mike had studied theology in Louvain, Belgium at the same time I was studying theology in Rome. He and I went to Holy Spirit High School Seminary together in Toledo, and to St. Meinrad College in Indiana. But it wasn't until we both considered going to Zimbabwe that our friendship blossomed. While we were still in the discernment process in Toledo, Mike and I would meet to talk about what we were experiencing, and the challenges with priesthood we faced. I enjoyed our conversations, and over the course of those months, he and I became good friends. Once Mike and Jules landed in the country, we spent a few days in Harare getting their residency papers organized. Then we took off for Bulawayo to meet the Franciscan Sisters and to shop at our favorite warehouse store. I got to see Mary again and introduced her to Mike. It was a quick trip, so we only had one evening together to talk. On the way to Hwange, Mike sat in the front seat of the Land Rover with me.

"Mary D is beautiful and a lot fun. No wonder you like her so much," he said and then winked.

I had told Mike about Mary shortly after he landed in Harare and he was looking forward to meeting her. We stopped in Hwange to meet more of the Franciscan Sisters and Bishop Prieto. Mike and I stayed at the convent with the other sisters. That evening Mike and I had a beer and were floating around alone in the convent's pool looking up at the brilliant night sky.

"Shane, this is great," he told me.

"Don't tell anyone else about this," I said, "everyone thinks we're suffering out here. Don't break the spell."

We had another beer. I loved these visits to the sisters in Bulawayo and Hwange because they provided a brief respite from the intensity of our life in Binga - just the three of us day after day. Mike and I sat in the front seat of the Land Rover as we drove out of Hwange and headed for Binga.

"So what am I supposed to do next, Shane?" He said.

"Just stay drunk for the next six weeks. After that, you can start becoming a missionary."

We both laughed, but that comment revealed more about my mental and emotional state than I realized. Just having Mike there was such a relief. Now I had someone I could talk to about what I was experiencing.

We arrived in Binga on February 13, 1986, and Mike and Jules moved into my house. Jules got a full bedroom while Mike got a smaller room we divided off from the sitting area.

For Mike and Jules to be of any use, they had to learn Tonga, and I became their instructor. I instituted the same discipline on them that worked for me: six hours a day of language study. That meant two hours with me in teaching and four hours of work on their own, mastering the grammar and memorizing words. It was grueling but essential work. The gazebo became our cool and breezy classroom. Occasionally a Tonga visitor stopped by, who would give my new students a chance to practice the language. The hardest thing for Mike, as it was for me in the beginning, was not to be busy. I told them that if they didn't learn the language, they were pretty useless in any kind of work except to children and they should think of themselves as children learning a new language and culture.

"Speak in simple declarative sentences," I told them.

Julitta joined our little language class since she had found learning Tonga difficult and after two years still struggled.

One day I gave them the assignment to write a short speech they would deliver at Mass the following week. They were nervous about this Tonga debut. Julitta, Mike, and Jules put in hours of work. The next Sunday they all delivered their little speeches in Tonga. When they finished, everyone applauded, and the bacembele ululated long and loud. Taking the risk to speak in Tonga to Tongas was the first step in connecting to their new surroundings both physically and emotionally. The Tongas made up a tiny fraction of the population, and they were expected to learn to speak English, Shona, and Ndebele which they did. Few of the whites or even Shonas bothered to learn Tonga, the language of the fewest and the poorest in Zimbabwe. Our effort signaled our willingness to become Tongas, and they embraced us as one of their own. Here we lived with people who teetered on the edge of starvation all the time, experienced disease and lived near wild animals who ate their grain and threatened their young. They found joy in simple things like dancing, singing, and connecting with nature, one another, and the ancestors who preceded them.

Mike was familiar with my challenges of loneliness in Binga as well as my struggles with being a priest. He told me that when he and the Bishop had visited a year before they were both concerned about me and the health of the team. They could see how depressed I looked and withdrawn from the sisters and how I avoided any kind of confrontation. Each evening after our Mass and supper, Mike and I sat outside my house under the stars to talk. I felt that I could share my deep distress about the priesthood. We found a perfect place, far enough from the others that we could talk openly. It stayed warm outside late into the evening. Without city lights, the stars of the Southern Hemisphere glimmered. Sitting with a couple of glasses of brandy under a canopy of the bright night sky, I talked, and Mike listened. For the first time, I poured out my heart to someone who knew me, knew my situation, and was willing to listen and support and challenge me. Over the next few months, Mike and I talked about our mutual struggles with celibacy and ministry in Binga.

"Mike, I've only just met Mary. But I think I'm in love with her," I told him. It was the first time I'd said those words, and it wouldn't be the last.

"I knew that the first time I saw you two together," he said.

We laughed and talked and reminisced late into the night almost every evening.

We adopted the phrase from the movie Ghost Busters: "We came. We saw. We kicked ass." It was Mike's way of humorously challenging me to begin to confront what I had been avoiding.

Somehow, the thought of not being able to live up to that simple motto of ours became a great motivator to deal with things. One morning Mike used our motto to challenge me to talk to Marge about something she'd said. She was in the kitchen making lunch. I told her how I felt. Marge listened and told me she didn't realize that it bothered me that much. And that was it. After years of distress, I thought to myself; I have been going through all of this needless suffering when all I needed to do was to say what I felt! The Bishop had said the same thing to me on both of his visits, but I had perfected avoidance after years of avoiding my feelings about being a priest. Swallowing my true feelings seemed easier than confronting them. Mike's challenge had started me on a different path.

Slowly, with Mike's support and encouragement, I became more comfortable with confrontations. The team was bigger, and the challenges and demands we faced now were different than when we first arrived. In the first two years of our time in Zimbabwe, there were many concrete things to get done. Marge's strong-willed determination had been crucial in establishing the Mission of Accompaniment. We lived in our own houses, and our outstations were increasing. We established a connection with the other priests and sisters who worked in the country. Her willpower, refusal to give up, and sheer determination helped us overcome many, many obstacles and road blocks. But a different vision for the team was emerging that was more collaborative and involved independent work which was creating problems. And so the confrontations continued to increase. A storm was brewing.

(Photo: Me in action)

Chapter 17

Mary Visits Binga August 1986

O n the next visit to Bulawayo Mary told me that she had some vacation time to use in August and she wondered if she could come to
Binga to see our mission. I was thrilled.

"This will be a great opportunity to see what mission life is like in the
bush, away from the city," I told her. I also thought this would be a chance
for us to have more time alone together.

"I would love to come. I have to clear it with Eileen first."

Sr. Eileen was the superior of the convent in Bulawayo who approved
her request. Mike and Jules would be in language school in Zambia. Julitta
would be in Hwange on a private retreat with the sisters and Marge, and I
would be on our own in Binga that week of August. So Mary and I could
have plenty of time to be together, and she could sleep in Julitta's bedroom
in Marge's house. The timing couldn't have been better. I became more
excited as the day drew nearer. Mary arrived in Hwange on the coach
from Bulawayo where I met her and brought her out to Binga. We talked
so much on the bumpy, dusty road to Binga that the drive, which always
seemed to take forever, flew by.

That evening Marge prepared a feast for us, and we had drinks on my front porch. Afterward, Mary and I took a walk and watched the sun go down over the lake. We held hands as we walked and when I dropped her off at Marge's house, she gave me another little kiss. The next day we drove out to two of the outstations we started near Binga on the corrugated sandy road. About 5 miles outside of town we turned onto an unmarked track. "How did you know to turn here? I didn't even see this road," she said.

"I've been here a few times before. I looked for the Baobab tree on the left side of the road as my landmark," I told her.

We crept along the track dodging huge potholes and listening to the branches scrape along the side of the Land Rover as we picked our way along. Then in the distance, we heard drumming and people singing. As we rounded a bend in the track the little school came into view, and we saw a crowd of men, women, and children singing, dancing, and waving to us. As I brought the Land Rover to a stop right in front of the school, the drumming stopped, and the old women began ululating. Mary jumped down and joined me as the people crowded around us. The leader of the village welcomed us, and I introduced Mary to him in Tonga, and we chatted for a few minutes. I felt proud to show off my ability to speak in Tonga. Then Mary and I greeted every single man, woman, and child with a handshake and a hearty "Mwabuka." Mary had been studying Ndebele in Bulawayo, and I taught her the greeting in Tonga and the handshake before we left Binga, and she did it like a pro. After we greeted each person we walked into one of the classrooms and Mary sat with the women. The drummers took their place in the front with me. I put on my white robe, sat at the teacher's desk, and everyone sat at desks or on the floor. It was all quiet for a moment. Then I nodded to the drummers who began to play and for a second everyone was on their feet swaying back and forth waiting for the song. The song leader began a chant, and everyone joined in the singing. The swaying evolved into some simple steps that the whole crowd did in unison, like the line dancing I had done at my sister's wedding. The drumming became intense, and the people added harmonies as the song evolved. We sang and danced for 15 minutes with the old women ululating right on beat. And then the drumming slowed and stopped and everyone sat down smiling and expectant.

I stood and greeted the whole crowd, "Mwabuka."

Everyone responded together, "Mwabuka Bafada" (Hello Father).

I looked out and saw a sea of faces smiling and Mary beaming, and my heart laughed with delight. After I had spoken about the light of God's love for them I sat down for a minute, the drummers started in, and everyone jumped to their feet. We sang and prayed for the next 2 hours. After it was over, we climbed back into the Land Rover to drive to our next outstation.

"I've never experienced anything like that ever. How did you learn to speak Tonga so well? What did you tell them all?" Mary was glowing.

As we picked our way along the track, I told Mary what I said and translated some of the songs for her. At our next stop, we experienced more of the same. It was dark by the time we finished the second visit. As we drove toward Binga, I suddenly stopped the car and turned off the lights.

"What are you doing?" Mary said. She seemed a little nervous.

"I am waiting until that herd of elephants crosses the road and gets into the bush."

"What elephants?" She said.

"There are at least six elephants ahead, and I think a few of them are young," I said.

"There's nothing there," Mary said.

"Ok. I am going to turn on the lights just briefly so you can see them. But if they get startled they might charge us, and I have to be ready to get out of here. Look at the road about fifty yards ahead."

I waited a moment and then turned on the lights. There on the road were at least ten elephants.

"Turn off the lights. Turn off the lights." Mary said.

"Looks like you saw them."

We waited for fifteen minutes, and when the road cleared, we continued on our way. I felt my love for Mary growing in this wild, exotic, and tropical place.

The next day I declared a day off, and I took Mary to an isolated beach on Lake Kariba. We drove on a dirt track about 3 kilometers outside of Binga, then walked through a forested area and down a steep hill to the beach. It felt like we were on a desert island. We found a sandy spot and laid out our beach towels and the food and drink we brought for the day. It was awesome to be sitting together looking out at the blue water of Lake Kariba, the clear sky and soft sand with no one around. Her skin looked so white and soft. Occasionally she caught me staring at her.

"What are you looking at?"

I was a little embarrassed, "You."

She smiled and gave me a peck on the cheek. The air at this time of the year was warm but not stifling. As we walked hand in hand on the beach, I felt an electricity. Her hand felt good in mine. I stopped walking, and she turned and looked up at me. I bent down and kissed her. She smiled. We walked a little further, and I stopped again and kissed her again. I felt her arms wrap around me and we held each other in a long embrace. She kissed me, and this time it was long and passionate. It was like an ice flow breaking up in a river of passion. It felt wonderful. After that, we took a deep breath and walked along this time holding hands a little tighter and walking a little closer than before. After we had eaten lunch on the beach, we stretched out on the blanket. I rolled onto my side to look at Mary laying there. She looked beautiful laying close to me in her swimming suit. We had broken so many rules in the past hour and the one we feared to break lurked on the edge of our beach towels. I leaned toward her, and we kissed again. I began to lose control when in the midst of a deep and passionate kiss, I heard some shuffling sounds near the forest. I looked up and saw a Tonga man walking along the edge of the woods. He stopped and looked at us, clapped his hands together and shouted out a friendly, "Mwabuka," he said, clapping his hands together and smiling. Then he disappeared up the hill.

The spell was broken. The beach wasn't quite as deserted as I thought. I wondered if the man was a member of the church. Mary found this quite funny and laid there giggling. Pretty soon we were both laughing. We spent the rest of the afternoon talking and splashing each other as we walked arm in arm along the lake's edge. When we arrived back at our houses, we found Marge sitting outside of her house, in the middle of the path that leads to my house. I had never before seen her sitting in this spot at the back of her house.

"So how was your day out?" She asked us. The look on her face was clearly one of disapproval. It put a cold chill through the both of us that dampened some of the passion we'd been experiencing. Marge was the acting "mother superior," worried about where my relationship with Mary was going. I could tell she thought it was dangerous. Marge was right, of course.

The week ended with a candlelight dinner down at the Safari Camp. We sat at a table outside in the fresh evening air, cool enough that Mary put on a sweater. I had ordered a bottle of wine and a three-course steak dinner. We could smell the fragrance of bougainvillea and hear the soft sounds of insects near the lake. After the waiter poured I wine we toasted each other. She caught me just staring at her again.

"What are you thinking?" She said.

"I love you."

"Oh my! I think I love you too," she said.

I reached across the table, and we held hands and sipped wine. We felt content and comfortable with each other. What else did we need to say? We walked for a while after dinner in the cool of the night and the anonymity that the darkness afforded. The only light I saw was the brightness of the moon reflecting off the lake and onto her beautiful white skin.

When I took Mary back to the convent in Hwange, I felt a mixture of gratitude for the time we'd spent together and of loss since we didn't know when we'd be together again. We loved the long hours alone together in Binga. In Bulawayo or Hwange, our times together would be few and far between.

In October the team went to Bulawayo for shopping. Mary and I had so much to talk about now, and we couldn't wait to see each other. But at the same time we had to be very discreet, so we never sat together at any meal in the convent, and I tried to make sure I mixed with all the other sisters. Occasionally I caught her smiling at me and saw her wink, and my heart melted.

Sometimes we talked about how she came to make the decision to join the convent or how I decided to become a priest. Mary told me one evening as we sat in the courtyard at the convent in Bulawayo that her mum and dad were very devout, the Catholic church was the center of the universe for them. Her mum and dad believed that if one of their children was given a vocation to be a priest or sister that made them successful Catholic parents.

When Mary graduated from the Catholic high school run by the Franciscan Sisters of the Divine Motherhood (FMDM), she told me that she began thinking about becoming a nun then. These sisters operated convents all over the world. The thought of going to England and seeing the world seemed so much more attractive than marrying a farmer, settling down, and having a big family. Encouraged by her parents, she convinced herself that she wanted to join the convent.

As she talked more and more about becoming a nun, she started to get the attention of the other Catholics in her hometown of Nathalia, Victoria. She loved the idea of traveling to other parts of the world, she loved the notice people gave her, and she loved the idea of a whole new life.

In October 1970 Mary applied to join the convent, and in February 1971 she moved in with the sisters in Bendigo, Victoria where she lived for four months. In June, when she was just 19 years old, she decided that she wanted to become one of the FMDM sisters. Mary flew to the FMDM convent in Godalming, England and in October 1971 became a Novice. It was the first time in her life that she had been on an airplane. Her training as a novice involved two years of intense study and prayer and little contact with the outside world. Other novices were from Asia, Rhodesia, Ireland, Scotland, USA, India, and there was a girl from London who was West Indian. Life was very structured and strict: silence most of the time, with talking allowed two hours a day, and the topics of conversation were highly regulated.

Mary settled into this life for two years. In the second year, she began to work as a nurse's aide in the hospital that the sisters ran. She found that she missed her family being so far from home. Her youngest sister, Regina, was born during this time. The "Rule" all the sisters followed discouraged any relationship that was close or intimate, even a friendship. They considered these relationships as dangerous since passions could flare.

"Save your intimacy for the Divine," her superiors told her. "Channel all your ability for love and affection to a spiritual love. Sacrifice yourself for others. Prayer is all the intimacy you need."

Mary learned it all but found no joy in it. She just went through the motions.

At the same time, she enjoyed the community and the friends she was making from all over the world. It never occurred to her that she could leave and do something else. Her focus was on keeping the Rule which defined everything from what the sisters wore, to the schedule of the day, to the type of work they did, to the relationships they could have. It was most important to obey the church. Following the Rule, she was told, brought joy. In the past few years she had begun to question her decision, but like me, she felt bound to the vows she made as a young person.

"Make the best of it." Her counselors told her.

Our shopping trips to Bulawayo only occurred every two or three months, and since we didn't have a phone in Binga, Mary and I wrote letters to each other. I wrote to her every Sunday and couldn't wait for her response. As we planned our next trip to Bulawayo, I would write to Mary to let her know so she could take her day off while I was there. Once all of the team's shopping or car repair business was taken care of, Mary and I felt free to be together. The team spent so much time together every day in Binga that in Bulawayo we left each other alone to do as we pleased. While Mary and I spent an afternoon or an evening out together, the rest of the team watched TV with the other sisters or caught a movie in the city. Mary and I always planned an evening out at one of our favorite restaurants in Bulawayo. For a town in Africa, Bulawayo had an amazing array of restaurants serving cuisines from Spanish to Italian to Lebanese to French. At one Italian restaurant, the waiter asked us if we were celebrating anything. I told him that we were celebrating our 12-month anniversary of meeting one another. A little while later, an announcement came over the speaker, "We are happy to announce that Mike and Mary are celebrating their first anniversary. Congratulations!" Then they played a song - "Happy Anniversary to You" - and the waiter presented us with a small cake and candle. Mary started to giggle. And after the waiter left we laughed and laughed. We laughed a lot whenever we were together.

Our visits to Bulawayo only lasted a few days, and each time we left, I felt more and more as if I left my heart there. Often Mary and I talked about how we could manage our deepening love for one another while at the same time staying faithful to our commitments. We wondered how we could balance these promises with this friendship and love we felt for one another.

On a ride back to Binga from one of our trips to Bulawayo, Marge had questioned whether I would tell her first if I planned to "run off" with Mary.

She said, "Some of the sisters talked to me about your relationship with Mary. They are concerned that it is becoming exclusive. Mary looks like she is in love with you." I didn't say anything. "Mike, would you tell me first if you planned to 'run off' with Mary?"

"First of all, I am not planning to 'run off' with Mary. And secondly, I would tell Bishop Hoffman first." I felt irritated that Marge wanted to be the first to know and I felt a little exposed that the other sisters expressed concern to her about my relationship with Mary. What Marge said was true. Mary and I were in love. Marge didn't like the answer and asked me again, the same question. "Bishop Hoffman would be the first to know," I told her. After that, we didn't speak much for the rest of the ride to Binga.

As my relationship with Mary began to flower, my life in the mission was blooming as well. On one of my visits to Nakangala, a man with leprosy and his wife invited me for supper. The wife prepared for me a special bowl with the cooked liver of the goat.

"This is for my child," she said as she handed me the bowl.

I realized that this childless woman regarded me as her son. All along I had felt like a child in the midst of these Tongas, and now this old woman adopted me as a son. In Kalungwizi, where I spent two weeks in my first year in Binga, the people there began to call me Mumuni, which means "light," since I always talked about the light of the love of God. Maybe God wasn't the enemy after all? I was experiencing something new, different, and freeing. The dark clouds of loneliness and isolation now began to dissipate in the light of the love I felt for Mary, the friendship I felt with Mike and Jules, and the relationships I had formed with the people. I felt lighter and more alive. But on the other hand, the confrontations in the team were happening with greater frequency; the clash of which vision for our work was right. And it was all about to come to a head.

Chapter 18

Marge Departs October 1986

———

This new vision for the team focused more on individual passions rather than group work. At the beginning Marge, Julitta, and I were happy to do everything together because there was so much to do and we were all trying to figure things out together. That took some getting used to as I was more accustomed to working independently. But because there was so much to do I put my own ideas on hold in order to get the mission established. It wasn't easy. But now that we had cleared all of the major hurdles in establishing the mission it seemed time for a change. Mike wanted to work more with Dr. Philip at the hospital. Jules liked to spend time with other young ex-patriots in the compound and sometimes came in late. Julitta had begun to develop women's sewing groups. These weren't big things, but our close-knit living situation magnified even the smallest problem.

Around this time Bishop Hoffman wrote a letter to Marge objecting to Jules' living situation. She was living in the house with Mike and me. When Marge, Julitta, and I planned the housing for Mike and Jules, we designed one house for team meetings, Mass, and dinner (Marge and Julitta's House) and the other subdivided to include an additional bedroom (my house). Though the living situation was unusual and from the outside seemed improper, Jules felt comfortable with Mike and me. Mike and I were like uncles to her. But Bishop Hoffman was not happy at all about the arrangement, and in his letter, he ordered Marge to rearrange the living situation so that women lived in one house and the men in the other. Marge brought it to the team.

"Well, what do you think we should do about this letter from Hoffman?" She said.

No one said anything. We all liked the living arrangements.

"Does anyone have an idea?" Marge asked us again. No one spoke.

"I think we should leave things as they are and see what happens," Mike said.

"Fine. I'm not going to respond to this letter for now." Marge said.

We ignored his order. What was he going to do about it anyway, being an entire continent and a whole hemisphere away?

One evening, Jules decided to go to a party with some young Dutch volunteers who lived near our house in the compound. Mike and I enjoyed our usual drinks out under the stars, and then went to bed. The next morning, I got up and made coffee. As I was pouring my first cup, Jules walked in the back door just getting home from her "all-nighter." We looked at each other.

"Jules?" I said.

"Mike?" she responded.

And that was that.

In late October 1986, Marge realized the tension in the team wasn't getting any better and that she had accomplished what she had come to do in establishing the mission. She told us it was time for her to leave Zimbabwe. Marge announced her date of leaving, packed her bags, arranged for transport to Hwange, and one Sunday was gone. Jules moved over to the women's house, the team reformed, and in a backward way, Bishop Hoffman's demand was fulfilled.

Mike and I moved our late night chats from the back of the house to the front porch where we sat in our underwear in the warm night air and drank beer.

Chapter 19

A New Vision November 1986

———————

S o began the next phase of our life in Binga.

Mike became involved in work at the hospital. He had earned his emergency medical technician certificate while living in Toledo and took vacation days to work in emergency rooms there. Mike loved medicine. Now he felt free to use his EMT training to help Dr. Philip at the hospital whenever he had time and without worrying about asking for permission.

Jules found her passion in sewing, and her women's sewing group began to grow. Like the rest of us, Jules embodied the ideal of our Mission of Accompaniment – to learn with the people as we helped them. She learned to sew right along with the rest of the women who embraced her as a daughter. Her box of sewing materials burst with donations she received from Toledo, and soon it contained more sewing goods than most stores in the country. The women sold their projects, turning Jules' little sewing circle into a micro-enterprise.

The mission at Kariangwe, where we'd spent four months three years earlier, asked us to take over their church in Kamitivi. Bishop Prieto and Bishop Hoffman agreed.

Julitta volunteered to take the challenge. "Now I can have a ministry of my own where I feel useful," she said. Julitta worked in parishes all over the USA before becoming part of the mission team. "This seems like I am becoming a real missionary."

A few weeks later she moved into a house near the church. Kamitivi was an hour and a half from Binga on the way to Hwange and Bulawayo. The parish included ex-patriots and people from all over Zimbabwe who worked in the tin mines there. Most people spoke English. Julitta was excited about leading the service and preaching. Mike volunteered to work with her and went to Kamitivi two weekends a month to say Mass. The rest of the time Julitta lived on her own. She felt lonely away from the team, so she adopted a dog whom she named "munkala," which is the Tonga word for dog. We all found that hilarious. Julitta also enjoyed electricity, hot water, and running water all the time. We planned trips to Kamitivi for team meetings and luxuriated in her amenities.

I started a garden in between our two houses. Gardening was not easy in the hot climate and sandy soil of Binga. Mike and I dug deep trenches and then filled them with the manure we hauled from the corrals at the Safari Camp down near the lake. I planted fruit trees all around my house and looked forward to eating my fresh vegetables and fruit someday. I created a compost pile that measured 30 feet long and 10 feet wide. My first garden produced such an abundance of eggplants that after months of eating them we all groaned if eggplant appeared on the menu.

"Today we have melanzana a la parmigiana for supper," I said one evening. I used the Italian I learned while studying in Rome.

"Wait a minute," Jules said, "this tastes like eggplant."

Busted! I planted pumpkins and agreed to let the teachers who lived nearby use the leaves as relish for their nsima. They harvested so many leaves over the next weeks that pumpkins never developed. At least I was feeding the hungry.

I counted the days until I would see Mary again and tried not to think about the fact that it would be months before I would get to see her. Sometimes I'd think about how nice it would be to come home to Mary every day from a regular job. Then I'd look around and realize how unlikely that scenario was. For now, I could only wait until we could see each other in Bulawayo for a few days every few months to cram in everything I wanted to tell her. Our weekly letters would have to suffice.

Our gazebo became a meeting place for the ex-patriots living in Binga, as well as a stopping-off point for people traveling from the bush. We decided not to give away food or clothing to people, but we invited anyone who stopped by to eat with us. We hired a cook and housekeeper who prepared one big main meal a day, washed clothes and ironed, and cleaned our houses. She cooked for us and for anyone who visited; nsima and a delicious relish that often included my specialty -- dried kapenta (sardine-like fish that were put in a brine and then dried) cooked in a tomato and onion sauce.

Word spread quickly as more and more people got to know us, and the number of people attending our services in Nakangala increased so much so that many people had to stand outside out little church structure when we had Mass. We needed something bigger and more permanent there to replace the grass-thatch and mud-walled structure that was quickly deteriorating. We planned to build a space for Sunday Mass and as a conference center where we could talk to people about church-related activities as well as about economic development projects. It would provide a central meeting place for everyone at the eastern end of our mission territory. Bishop Hoffman agreed to pay for the concrete floor, steel girders, and a roof. The people of Nakangala decided to make the bricks.

I went out on my own to the outstations for four or five days at a time, enjoying my time away but also looking forward to returning to our team life together in Binga or Kamitivi. Whenever we got together, everyone was bursting with news and developments whether it was the increasing number of women coming to Jules's sewing groups, Mike's hospital work, or my stick figure teaching programs. We were all full of life and energy. We got a surprise visit one day from the people of Malube who sent a small delegation of leaders to Binga. Our cook prepared a feast of nsima and kapenta for us all. We gathered in the gazebo sitting around the table on carved wooden stools we were continually buying from people who sold them to make extra money.

After we had finished eating, the leader of the group stood up in a very formal manner and addressed us, "Bafadas and BaJulie," he started, "we have been coming together every week to pray as Catholics. We are longing to learn the rosary and to take communion. We have decided that we want to become Catholic. We want to join the church." He went on, "We have seen the other Catholics taking communion, going to confession, and wearing their rosaries everywhere and we want to be part of that now. What do we have to do?"

Mike and I never pushed joining the church on any of our visits. Their request surprised us. "It will take a year of study," I said.

"Fine. Let's get started," the leader told us.

So the next Sunday I went with Jules out to Malube where, after Mass, I asked everyone, "How many of you want to go through a year of learning to become Catholic?" Everyone's hand shot up and the bacembele ululated. Jules looked at me and smiled. She already knew most of the women since they were regular members of her sewing group. Jules had been an inspiration for them. Her simple act of learning to sew with them resulted in their wanting to know more about Jules' faith.

The Bishop had told us before we left that we didn't have to focus our attention on making everyone Catholic. "Shane, take the time to walk in their shoes and leave it up to the 'Big Guy' to show you the next step. Let Him drive once in a while," he said.

Our code word for God was 'The Big Guy,' and the Bishop, on more than one occasion, encouraged me to relax a little and let God "drive once in a while." The Bishop wanted us to spend time understanding the Tonga life and culture, and giving them a hand up out of a fragile existence that threatened starvation with every poor rainy season. Now people came to us and asked us, on their own, to fully participate in the church.

I needed something written in Tonga that explained the teachings of the faith. The only thing we had was an old question/answer manual that one of the priests had written decades earlier. I decided to write a book in Tonga that included scripture sharing as an essential component of the class. When we first arrived in Binga, Bible Sharing helped us to get to know people better, and now I wanted to incorporate this into the way that we talked about faith in God. I wanted to know what they already believed. Bible sharing would give us another opportunity to learn more about people's everyday lives.

A week later we were driving to Hwange for supplies, and we stopped off in Dette, just near the big Safari Game Park. The Spanish Sisters had a convent there, and I'd heard about one of their African Sisters who was an artist. I met with her in the convent's lounge and explained my book concept. She ran to her room to get her portfolio of drawings, and we slowly paged through her art. She seemed thrilled to be part of this project. I realized that she had already done most of the work. I wanted to open each class with singing and dancing; something everyone loved, followed by prayer and a brief teaching, a Scripture reading and a chance for people to talk about the meaning of a Bible verse, then more singing, and then a closing prayer. A session like this might last two hours. Everything in the lesson reinforced the theme, from the songs we sang to the illustrations in the book. I knew the old women would never be able to read, but they could understand the Sister's picture and explain the meaning of what they heard. I worked on each lesson for hours Monday through Wednesday. As I completed the project, I invited some of the leaders from our outstations to check my Tonga.

Whenever we went to Hwange for our shopping trips, we now stopped first in Kamitivi for the night to re-enter the world of running water and electricity. Then the next day all four of us would go to Hwange and spend a few days with the sisters there enjoying their swimming pool and dinners at the Baobab hotel. The gorge outside of Kamitivi still thrilled us. Mike and I became more daring with each visit competing to see how fast we could go down into the gorge, and if we could make it up the other side in third gear. On one occasion I had a great run timing the curves perfectly to maintain speed. I was flying along when the latch on the front hood came loose, and the hood flew up blocking my view at a critical moment. Now I was flying blind.

Mike yelled out, "SHIT!"

I crouched down in the seat and could see enough of the road between the bottom of the hood and the top of the engine while Mike stuck his head out of the passenger window shouting instructions.

"Shane, you're getting close to the edge. I can see the river. Pull to your left NOW!"

With so little of the road visible I slowly drifted to the left and then back to the center. The Land Rover was so unstable that I slowly pumped the brakes, downshifted into second gear, and eventually guided the vehicle to a stop just as we reached the bridge. I sat for a moment, looked over at Mike and said, "Buddy, we are going to the Baobab Hotel for a couple of Carltons before we get into Hwange." We double fastened the hood this time and crawled up the gorge in first gear, glad to be alive. We stopped at the Baobab hotel, found a table in the garden outside and enjoyed a fried chicken basket and a few Carlton Beers. Relaxing on the outdoor patio under the huge Baobab tree looking out over miles and miles of savannah with a few Carlton's, a basket of fried chicken, and french-fries was pure bliss.

The team went to Bulawayo every six to eight weeks, depending on our supply needs and the state of the Land Rover which, since the accident, always needed some repair. During these trips, Mary and I spent as much time together as we could. Everyone on the team knew that Mary and I were becoming close friends. I think the sisters hoped it wouldn't escalate into something more passionate.

Mary and I took one afternoon to go to a national park near Bulawayo called Matopos. It preserved hundreds of miles of forest that contained beautiful rock outcroppings and many ancient rock paintings. We hiked through the park with our lunch, looking for the perfect place to spend an afternoon. We loved Matopos because we could find an isolated place on top of one of the ledges where we didn't have to worry about being discovered. It was quiet. The rocks were stacked hundreds of feet high, and the Bush gave the place both a primitive and enchanted feel. Trails wound for many kilometers through the park. We climbed onto a rocky ledge and spread out our blanket. Sitting there alone, it felt like we were on top of the world. After lunch, we laid down next to each other listening to the sounds of the birds and the wind in the trees. My heart beat faster as we held hands and kissed. I didn't want it to end. Then after lunch and a little nap, we hiked through the park together. On another visit we walked into the depths of the park and came out in a different place than where we began, trying to find our way back. I took off in one direction, while Mary went the other. I tried to convince Mary to come my way.

"I'm going this way. You can go where you like. I'll wait for you when I get to the car," she said.

In a rare moment of clarity, I turned and followed her. In a short time, we were back in the car and motoring into the city.

Mary loved our adventures out to Matopos where danger lurked from ZAPU guerrillas and wild animals. The police often set up roadblocks on our way out to Matopos. They were searching for ZAPU guerrillas and regularly stopped us and searched our car for weapons. When we were alone, she expressed her affection for me in a hug or a kiss.

We stole time to take walks together in the evening around the grounds of the convent and hospital. There never seemed to be enough time to be together. Neither of us felt fulfilled in our vocations, but we didn't know how to leave the lives we'd chosen, or how we'd turn our backs on our vows. We invested significant time and effort into this church-life, and we feared the distress and disappointment our leaving would cause to others. I found it difficult since I had become so well known in the Toledo Diocese.

While getting ready to leave for Zimbabwe, one of my colleagues said, "I'm going to miss reading about you in the Chronicle."

The Catholic Chronicle, the local Catholic newspaper regularly printed stories about me while I lived in Toledo. Now there were even more about my adventures in Zimbabwe. I was a celebrity. Leaving the priesthood would be a scandal. Besides, I didn't have any marketable skills. How could I support myself or a family?

One evening Mary asked me if I had ever thought about leaving the priesthood.

"I quit the seminary at least twice during my studies," I said, "but someone kept talking me into staying. Since ordination, I always thought it was too late, and I would just have to live with it." Then I asked, "Have you ever thought about leaving the convent?"

"I never considered it," she answered, "I've enjoyed lots of opportunities since becoming a sister. I trained as a physical therapist. I traveled to Rome and studied there for a year. Now here I am in Zimbabwe." Then she asked me if I liked being a priest.

"I like certain parts of it like preaching and teaching. I like having the time to pursue meditation and a deeper spirituality. I like the people I get to meet, like you. I've been all over the world. But no, I don't like being a priest. It's lonely," I said.

"I'm not that fond of convent life either," she told me.

We held hands for a while not knowing what to say next. We were both confused and unsure.

Back in Binga, I continued to write long letters to Mary every Sunday detailing the happenings of the week and my love for her. During those writing sessions, I felt close to her. The letters became a lifeline for me. They were a way of connecting with her in the city while I lived six hours away in the bush.

(Photo: Mike, Julitta, Jules, and me on my front porch in Binga)

Chapter 20

The Rhino November 1986

O ur new church building in Nakangala progressed with the steel girders, the concrete floor, and the roof now in place. Over the past month, the people of Nakangala burned a few large stacks of bricks and Mike, Jules, and I decided to take a long weekend to help move them from the oven to the church building site. Julitta came from Kamitivi to join us.

It was a Thursday morning in late November when we took our two vehicles out to Nakangala. After we had unloaded our gear into our thatched, mud-walled rondavels, we drove out to a field to start loading bricks from the stacks about a mile from the church site. Julitta and I drove the Land Rover and pulled a small open trailer which we had purchased from a Portuguese expatriate, a member of Julitta's church in Kamitivi. The people had spent the past two months digging clay and baking it into bricks, which required lots of skill and we were all impressed when we saw four tall stacks. We all got busy loading them into the trailer. So much work had gone into forming and burning the bricks that we all treated each one as if it were a bar of gold. Everyone chatted away at how strong they were and how well-made. With the basic structure of the church in place, we were on our way to finishing the church. We'd filled the trailer and were getting ready to haul the first load to the church when we noticed that most of our group was standing off in the distance staring at something in a nearby field. No one spoke. Following their gaze, we saw that something had been watching us - a huge rhinoceros. Its front horn stood out from its massive armored body. The next moment people began to run. Some ran to their villages and others jumped into the Land Rover. The four of us took off in our two vehicles; the Land Rover with the trailer bumping along behind us in the rough field and the newer Toyota Land Cruiser. We drove the mile back to the church on the main road and hoped that the rhino would wander back into the game reserve that surrounded the area. Rhinos typically stayed in the deep bush and never came close to the villages.

Once at the church, we began offloading bricks, but fifteen minutes later we heard people shouting and a sound like a drum beating on the road. The same rhino was charging down the road. Thursday was "Chief's Day" or a day off, and many people took this opportunity to visit friends and family, walking from village to village, unwittingly exposing themselves to this unexpected threat.

Mike looked at me and said, "We've got to do something."

"You and Jules go to get the police and Julitta, and I will take off after the rhino," I said.

Mike and Jules drove the Land Cruiser with a few people to the nearby police camp. The police owned few vehicles, and there were no phones, but they did have rifles which we thought could come in handy to scare or shoot the rhino. Julitta and I and a few of the men took off after the Rhino in the Land Rover.

The Rhino hadn't gotten far before someone spotted it running ahead of us on the right side of the road.

"I have to get in front of it so we can warn people," I told everyone. "I'm going to go around it."

No one spoke. I began to accelerate and move to the left, hoping the rhino wouldn't decide to veer over to my side of the road. No one said a word. At one point I looked over, and I saw its huge horn sticking up above the passenger window, while my passenger stared straight ahead, willing us to make it around. The vehicle crept forward, and as we passed it, a huge cheer erupted from the car. Just then the rhino caught sight of us and began to chase the Land Rover. As I sped ahead, everyone in the car shouted out to people on the road to run for their lives. Many people didn't understand or believe the warning until they saw the huge animal rumbling toward them, at which point they threw off whatever they carried and ran to their village. I stopped to pick up a few old women who couldn't move fast enough. We drove on for miles and miles, eventually driving up onto a hill that overlooked a valley. We stood near a tree on the top of the bluff looking out over the savannah. There in the middle of this peaceful place, the massive rhinoceros stopped. For a moment it almost looked like a scene some wildlife painter created, with the villages, the rugged hills, the baobab trees, and the huge rhinoceros standing there in the midst of it all.

From this vantage point we watched the beast until in the distance, we saw a plume of dust moving along the road, and we caught sight of Mike and Jules's Land Cruiser. The rhino stood in a blind curve. We feared Mike, Jules, and the police would ram into it. We started jumping and waving our arms in the air hoping to get Mike's attention. But he continued rumbling along. He couldn't see us. Mike came closer and closer, and then as he rounded the curve we saw the vehicle slam to a stop fishtailing a bit on the sandy road, and quickly reverse to a safe distance from the rhino. We saw the police step out of the Land Cruiser and creep closer to it, their rifles at the ready. They stopped. Suddenly shots rang out. The police fired into the air attempting to scare the rhino back into the bush, but it didn't move. The police continued to fire closer to the ground nearer the animal. We could see little clouds of dust rise as the bullets hit closer and closer to it. After ten minutes of shooting, the rhino, tired of the noise, ambled off into the bush. Relieved, Mike and I headed back to the church, picking up many of the men who came out to protect their villages from the rhino along the way. As they got into the Land Rover, we saw that they all carried spears. These brave men decided to risk their lives to defend their families against the attack of this mighty animal using only a stick with a metal point, much as their ancestors must have done thousands of years before.

Everyone talked about the rhino adventure for the rest of our time in Nakangala. At various gatherings in the future people would tell the story of our bravery in chasing it down. They embellished the story at each retelling, which always pleased the crowd. Our willingness to defend the villages endeared us to the people.

Chapter 21

Vacation, Malaria, and Home:
January – October 1987

———

I n January 1987, Mary and some of the sisters invited me to come with them to spend a ten-day vacation at a beautiful mansion in the Eastern Highlands of Zimbabwe. They liked the idea of having their priest along for their holiday so they could have Mass every day and I loved the idea of being on vacation with Mary for a couple of weeks - even if that meant sharing her with four other sisters. Mike and Jules loaned me the Land Cruiser for the week since it was the most dependable vehicle and the least likely to lose some of its parts on our journey. I arrived in Bulawayo on Monday after I finished celebrating Mass in the bush and we left early on Tuesday morning. Mary sat next to me on the front bench seat with another sister, and a third sat in the back of the vehicle on a small chair. Two other sisters came along in a car. We drove the 8 hours from the convent, past Harare and were soon driving into the highlands of Eastern Zimbabwe. The countryside was so different from the tropical landscape of Binga. This area was mountainous with pine forests, lakes and flowing streams. The home sat on the top edge of a deep ravine. It was built entirely of stone quarried from the area. At the bottom, a clear river flowed through the forests surrounding the house. Entering the house, we walked through a large kitchen and then into the Great Room with a massive fireplace. Windows along one wall looked out over a spectacular view of the mountains. A little wall and columns separated the Great Room from a hallway that ran along the back of the house like columns in an ancient Roman temple. Five bedrooms sat along the back of the house with the master suite at one end. The sisters gave me this big bedroom with a terraced patio attached, where I could sit in the morning with a cup of coffee. It would be a perfect place for me and Mary to be alone together too.

Fruit trees and berry bushes of all kinds grew on the terraces that stretched from the house down to the river. Staff lived in two-room stone homes, dotted throughout the orchards. The owner planted these orchards and berry patches to make and sell jam, and it happened to be "jamming" time during our visit. Every day a worker gave us a jar of whatever they made that day. The jam-cooking operation took place in a shed right outside the kitchen so that the odors from that sweet work wafted into the house mixed with the smell of pines and the fresh mountain air. I was in heaven.

Mary and I spent time hiking in the mountains and walking along the streams together. Whenever we took a hike, we invited the others to come along. Sometimes one of the other sisters joined us on our treks. But most of the sisters came there to rest, which meant sitting in the sun, reading a novel, or ambling up the lanes that surrounded the house. Mary and I wandered off on our own most days. We felt conflicted as we wanted to spend more and more time alone and at the same time feared where our passions might lead. The time alone gave us more chances to talk and explore the depth of our affection for one another, but the larger group of older sisters acted like gentle chaperones who provided limits to our alone time. If things got too "hot and heavy" we knew there was a safe space for us in the house.

On one of our walks, I asked Mary about her ideal life.

She thought for a long time as we walked in a pine forest, then looked at me and said, "In my teenage years, I loved the idea of living on a sheep station in Australia. Then I thought I would enjoy joining the convent and experiencing a wider world. Now I am not sure what I want." She looked at me and said, "What about you?" "Sometimes I wonder if I shouldn't have been a dentist. Then I could own a home with a white picket fence and have a big family. Right now that seems like an ideal scene to me." We stopped in the middle of the pines and held each other in a long embrace.

A few times we climbed fairly high mountains. One day we followed a narrow winding path up the side of a rocky outcropping a few hundred feet high. Mary couldn't wait to see what it looked like on top. As I looked up and saw that the narrow path disappeared at one of the higher points, I balked at the idea. But before I knew it Mary had vanished.

She yelled back to me over her shoulder, "You better get started. I'm going up."

What could I do? I caught up with her, and we picked our way up the steep and narrow path. At some places it was so narrow that we had to inch along, fearing that with one wrong step one us might fall hundreds of feet to a bloody end. I didn't dare look down. "Are you sure you want to keep going?" I asked her.

But she grunted something about I could do what I liked and kept climbing. She moved up the path like a mountain goat (a beautiful mountain goat) and then disappeared around the side of the mountain, as I inched my way along behind her I worried I'd find her splayed on the rocks hundreds of feet below.

As I poked my head around the edge of the rocks Mary said, "Boo," and then she started to giggle.

I felt smitten. When we reached the top, we discovered a flat, grassy plateau. It felt like we were standing on top of the world. Steep, rocky mountains towered above us and surrounded us on every side, but we stood in a meadow, lush with grass. At that moment, I felt as if my soul connected with hers and we held each other, breathless from the climb and the closeness we felt for one another. My heart beat faster as we held one another. Mary was adventurous, daring, and full of fun. I looked at her and said, "Darling." She looked up at me, smiled, and kissed me. We laid down in the grass together. We had faced the challenge of the climb together, but we still had no idea of how to face the challenge that our relationship posed to our vows.

Back at the house, we enjoyed making dinners, reading novels, and playing cards in the evening in front of the fireplace with the other sisters. Late one night, Mary and I sat alone near the fire after the others had gone to bed. She sat on my lap, and we kissed and watched the fire. The flames from the fireplace flickered against the walls and reflected light from the windows. Suddenly one of the sisters opened her door, and Mary dropped off my lap like a rock. Her sudden appearance and Mary's disappearance startled me, and I started to laugh, but Mary did not find the situation funny at all and glared. A few minutes later the sister called out, "good night," and went to bed. We both followed suit. The ten days passed quickly, and soon I was back in Binga, without her.

Life was changing for me. The dark thoughts I experienced during my first two years seemed to be evaporating. I enjoyed life with the team and the work in the outstations. I felt comfortable with the Tonga language and relieved that I didn't have to write out every single word I wanted to say. And I loved being with Mary. I loved the freedom to explore the work I enjoyed at the mission and to explore my friendship, intimacy, and love for Mary. As much as I loved the work and my new life in Binga, I loved being with Mary much more. When I got back to Binga later in January, I plunged into the work, but I left my heart in Bulawayo. My letters to Mary each week now began, "My Darling."

Malaria

In May of 1987, I contracted malaria for the third time, and unlike the
other two times, I couldn't shake it. A year earlier we changed the type of
anti-malaria pills we took because they were easier on the stomach and
more available. But in the past year, I got malaria twice. It felt like the flu
but with spiking fever fits called "the rigors" where my whole body shook.
The cure involved taking more anti-malaria medicine, but the "chills" kept
returning and sapping my strength. I laid in bed for a week getting weaker
and weaker. Mike and Jules wanted to send me to the hospital in Bulawayo
where Mary worked. I had never needed this level of care before. I worried
about my ability to recover. So many of the Tongas died from malaria.

After three weeks Mike ordered me to get packed. "You are going to the
hospital in Bulawayo. Besides, you can spend more time there with Mary."

The thought of spending more time with Mary convinced me. Mike
drove me to Bulawayo. I thought the change in climate and food would help
me to kick the disease, but I kept having spiking fevers. I became weaker
and weaker and wasn't even able to get to the dining room for dinner or to
tea time and Sr. Jacinta's pastry trolley. Mary sat at my bedside whenever
she had a free moment and made a point of coming into my room every
hour to take my temperature. The problem was that my fever kept spiking.
After a week, I could just manage to sit up or go to the bathroom. Mary
convinced me I needed to go to the hospital.

I laid in the hospital for almost a week. At one of the doctor's visits,
after asking me a few questions about my work, he looked straight at me
and said, "You don't like what you're doing at all. You're flat." And then he
walked out of my room.

I didn't know what to make of this. I felt "flat" because of malaria, I
thought. But the doctor saw something else. I exuded no excitement,
energy, or spark of enthusiasm when I talked about Binga. This doctor,
treating my malaria, correctly identified the deeper problem I faced: I

didn't like being a priest. While I loved the adventure of the Bush and the excitement of being in Africa, I wanted to have my family and a home.

Mary visited me often in the hospital. I did not have the energy to do much more than taking a walk around the grounds in the evening with her. Eventually, the doctor released me, despite the fact that the fever still spiked regularly. He told me to take three times the recommended dosage the next time I experienced the rigors. Mary was still worried about me. A few months earlier I had been climbing mountains with her, and now all I could do was to take short walks around the convent grounds. She wanted me to stay longer in Bulawayo, but I felt guilty being away from the mission for so long. Mike came to Bulawayo and drove me back to Binga, but I was still fragile. I waited for the rigors to appear. It wasn't long before my fever spiked and I was shaking all over. I downed 18 pills at once, as the doctor had instructed me, even though my stomach rebelled at taking so many of these pills at one time. To my great relief, the rigors stopped along with the spiking fevers. But I felt drained. The team continued to meet without me and talk about upcoming projects. Two weeks later I still spent most of my time sleeping, sitting out on our front porch, walking a little each day, and reading novels. I hoped that I could get strong enough to make the flight home for my scheduled four-month leave.

Home

By the end of June, I felt well enough to travel. While in the hospital in Bulawayo I told Mary how much I would miss seeing her while I stayed at home in the States for four months. It turned out that the date scheduled for my flight out of Harare coincided with a physical therapy conference she planned to attend in there. So, Mike, Jules, and Julitta brought me to Bulawayo in late June where Mary and I drove a car from Bulawayo to Harare. We stayed with the Dominican Sisters there who hadn't seen me since I'd stayed with them when I first arrived. They couldn't wait to hear about how the mission was going in Binga. Now I was a seasoned missionary. I said Mass for them every day and drove Mary to her conference.

That evening we went out to eat and spent more time together. The next morning, she drove me to the airport. We said our goodbyes and then she left for Bulawayo while I boarded my flight for home.

On the way home, I stopped in Munich for a few days to visit my cousins Muschi, Robert, and their two children Andrea and Manuela, whom I had visited a few years earlier with Marge. Still weak from malaria I spent most of the trip resting at their house or wandering out into Munich visiting familiar places. Then I flew to London to reconnect with Cardinal Hume whom I befriended at a retreat I had attended in Mystic, Connecticut in 1982. He drove me around London to look at the sights. After three and a half years in Zimbabwe, the stops in Munich and London felt like a slow reentry into the First World again, like a diver coming up from the depths of the ocean. I loved Europe, and it reminded me of my student days living in Rome. After a few days, I was ready to fly home.

As my flight neared the airport, I felt excited about seeing Mom and Dad and my family again. I heard a shout as they caught sight of me walking into the terminal. My ten-year-old nephew, Justin, came running up to me and couldn't wait to get his arms around me and I met my niece Shannon, who was a few months old. Zimbabwe seemed so far away. And for the moment I let my family shower me with love. I stayed at home for a few weeks, still low on energy from malaria. In the mornings I walked at the Metro Park nearby, took the time to rest, and slowly felt my strength return. I moved to the Cathedral in mid-July and made that my base of operations. I unpacked in my old room as if I had never left. I traveled all over the diocese talking about the mission. My celebrity grew. I flew around the country visiting friends in Tennessee, California, Colorado, Kentucky, and New Orleans. The effects of the malaria were gone, and I felt like my old self again. I loved the whirlwind tour and reconnecting with friends. During this time I said goodbye to women friends I knew from my time in Toledo and Tiffin. In my heart, I knew I'd found the girl I loved. I talked a lot to my good friend Terry about Mary and spent a good deal of my visit with him in LA shopping for her. I spoke to my brother Fred and my sister Janet about her and mentioned her again to the Bishop. I thought about her all the time. My weekly letters to Mary continued from Toledo. I lived between two worlds but didn't know how to reconcile them. I kept thinking about what that doctor had said to me, "You are flat." My problem existed in my heart. What held me back from jumping head first into this relationship? I had made a vow of celibacy and a promise to be a priest for the rest of my life at my ordination. But now I realized that these two commitments drained the life out of me. I felt that I couldn't turn my back on these promises or the many people in the parishes who held me in such high esteem. To walk out on my vows would be like turning my back on God. So instead of turning to Him for guidance, I began to think of Him as the enemy. I felt trapped in that awful decision. I'd met the girl I wanted to spend the rest of my life with and couldn't.

In mid-October, I flew back to Zimbabwe with a bag full of presents for Mary. I couldn't wait to get back – not to Binga, but to Mary. I arrived in Harare, took a flight to Victoria Falls and spent a few days there with her. I couldn't wait to show her everything I brought for her. In my room, I began to pull out all of the gifts I bought. I gave her eight cassettes of music she wanted from the list of classical music she received from a music appreciation course she took while in Rome. I brought her a scarf, some perfume to wear when we went out, tennis shoes, and a Sony Walkman for her tapes. She couldn't believe how much stuff I bought. We spent time at the Falls walking and talking. I loved being with her. But after a few days together, Mary had to leave for Bulawayo, and Mike and Jules came from Binga to take me back to the mission.

Chapter 22

Binga Part 2

D riving back to Binga with Mike and Jules I thought about all that had happened since I'd arrived three years before. Now a tar road reached almost all the way from Hwange to Binga which meant no more corrugations. We upgraded the old kerosene refrigerator, which rarely worked anyway, to a reliable gas model. Our solar panel charged a battery that ran florescent lights. We now had a telephone, and one day there we might have electricity.

A week after I returned from leave, Mike, Jules and I started talking about building a church in Binga to accommodate the growing attendance at Mass and the increasing number of people coming to our conferences. We completed the church in Nakangala, where we hosted many small meetings. But the number attending began to exceed the space available in the church. Binga was the center for government and for our mission station, and there were requests for us to build a bigger church and conference center. For the past few years, we called our mission, "The Binga Catholic Mission." One day after Mass some of the people approached us about giving our church a "proper name." We convened a group of the church leaders, and they decided to rename our mission - "All Souls" - to honor the ancestors the Tongas venerated.

At the same time, we decided to build the church in Binga, we also decided to replace the mud huts where we stayed in Nakangala. The number of outstations continued to grow, and the central location of Nakangala would be perfect for our base in that part of the mission territory. The current huts were deteriorating; the mud was falling off the walls, and the grass thatch needed attention. The two new homes would improve our life in the bush without being too flashy. We wanted to build each house in the round, with a concrete floor, a brick wall stuccoed with cement, a thick grass thatch for the roof, and two small windows. We wanted to make these homes comfortable enough so that one or two of us could stay there for a few weeks at a time.

In early November I met with some of the men to discuss our building plans in Nakangala. As we discussed the buildings, the men began to complain about the "mukuwa," the white people. The mukuwa never took the time to understand what the Tonga needed or to learn their language and culture. They drove up and down the road in big cars, especially the foreign aid workers who came out for a couple of years and then left. These Tongas never felt any better off as a result of the mukuwa coming to the area. I interrupted the conversation to remind them that I was a mukuwa.

They looked at me a little confused, and then one man said, "No, Syamuunda, you are Tonga."

I never knew how well I was connecting with people through my teaching, preaching, and visits. We had lived there for almost three years, spending most of that time learning the language and the culture and trying to identify what the people wanted to do. We hadn't accomplished much of what needed to be done to improve the life of these Tongas. But these men expressed appreciation for me and gave to me the highest honor I could ever expect; they regarded me as one of them. It felt good.

Other things were changing too. More families built homes in our little compound as government offices expanded and surrounded our cement block houses. We had neighbors. No more sitting on the front porch in our underwear. It felt good not to be so isolated and to be more integrated into this growing community.

We all got busier with our projects. One evening Mike had gone to the hospital to work with Dr. Philip, and Jules was meeting with her sewing group. I was alone in my house in Binga when a young European couple appeared on my front porch and asked for me by name. Frank Vermuellen and Hilde Buelens were part of a new group of international volunteers coming to Binga called "Cataruzi." I invited them in for a cold beer and something to eat. They seemed relieved not only to have found me but also that I drank beer. We had a great chat about Cataruzi. Frank and Hilde were both from Belgium, and Hilde planned to teach in the school while Frank looked for other work. They were looking for the Catholic priest since Cataruzi was a Catholic organization and the workers needed a Catholic sponsor wherever they went. I told them I would be glad to sponsor them here. Work began on their house in December and by the following March Hilde and Frank had moved into our growing compound community. Mike and Jules and I adopted them into our little mission family.

What a difference from the slow start Marge and I experienced when we first arrived! We had already built one new church and planned a second larger church and community center in Binga. We began to explore various development projects with the people - micro-enterprises that could bring them a better standard of living. Word spread among the women about Jules's sewing club, and soon Jules decided to form more of them. These sewing clubs produced beautiful hand made products which the women sold door to door or at the market. Since we stayed longer than other international volunteers, we were able to develop solid relationships with various local village leaders who could discuss with us what they wanted to do, not what we thought they should do. We began to explore getting donkeys, building grain mills, establishing fishing cooperatives, and growing new crops like cassava and cashews. Occasionally we traveled to Harare to talk to the staff at the American Embassy, who encouraged us to get something started. Based on the success of these smaller projects, the embassy staff told us they would be willing to give us some grants.

I kept feeling that I had one foot in Binga, with all its excitement of the growth of the mission and our acceptance among the people, and the other foot in Bulawayo where my affection for Mary grew stronger with every visit. In February 1988 I began to keep a daily journal to sort out the confusion of emotions and thoughts I was experiencing. Mike and I continued to talk about our mutual struggles with celibacy and our lives as priests. It felt great to have someone to talk to who didn't talk about the wonders of being a priest or tell me how good I was at it. The Tongas carried few expectations about how I should be and accepted me as one of them. If I shared a meal with them, they loved me. If I sang with them, they loved me. If I just walked quietly on my own, they loved me. Here in this remote outpost, I experienced few expectations. At one gathering the drummers asked me to lead a new song they had composed. I spent hours with them practicing it over and over again. On the day of my debut, I sang loud and clear and very off key. After the celebration, I apologized for my poor performance.

The head drummer laughed, "Yes. But you sang with such enthusiasm that we all joined in with you -- off key."

It felt so freeing. I wrote and sketched in my journal with a new purpose and the same sense of exuberance I experienced in 1983 as I tried to decide whether or not to go to Africa. I expressed my deepest thoughts, fears, and feelings in my journal where there was no critic and no editing, just the raw emotion and depth of feeling I experienced at that moment. As I wrote and sketched, I questioned my thinking and my decisions without censorship. I didn't know where this journaling would take me, but I began to express feeling and thoughts and emotions I had kept hidden from myself and everyone else for many years. It felt like something was starting to break free.

More and more people asked us to visit them. We decided to ask each community to choose leaders to meet with us for a few days. Thirty to forty people attended, and we taught them how to form small Christian communities so that they could lead them without us present.

The rainy season did not develop in late 1987, and by March 1988 we were in a severe drought. The crops of corn the Tongas depended on for food did not grow. Jules became involved in the relief efforts which consisted of the distribution of food to families and seeds for planting for the next season. We asked Jules to mobilize the women in her sewing groups to oversee the distribution of the cornmeal and seeds. Her women's sewing circles would make sure that they would get to the families that needed them the most. It was the tradition that the men took charge. This time there was too much opportunity for some of the supplies to go for beer or money. At first, they complained about this method, but since we had lived there for so long and they trusted us, those complaints were drowned out by other men in the villages who agreed with our plan. Jules' sewing groups now became strategy sessions. More and more women came to our houses, and the gazebo was the central point for planning. We cooked bigger meals to feed the number of women and their children who came to our gazebo to plan the distribution strategies with Jules. As the trucks from Bulawayo arrived with cornmeal and seeds sent by Catholic Relief, Jules and the women took charge. Jules rode shotgun in the truck while the women sat with the bags in the back. At each stop, people lined up to receive their allotment of food and seeds. Mike or I would follow the truck in the Land Rover, and we sat in amazement as these women efficiently handled the crisis. After a few weeks, all the supplies were exhausted. Jules had come into her own. Mike and I got out of her way.

Our homes in Binga became more and more a hub of activity. The garden produced magnificently. We ate eggplant, peppers, onions, and corn. Our fruit trees produced oranges, lemons, guava, and grapefruit. Mike got chickens, and it wasn't long before we were eating fresh eggs. Like the Tongas, we too were becoming self-sufficient.

Projects developed so quickly that Mike, Jules, and I soon felt over-whelmed. Bishop Hoffman agreed to give us additional funds to hire someone to help us. In June we hired Frank as our Project Development Coordinator, and he jumped in with both feet. Frank couldn't believe his luck and neither could we. He took on the responsibility of building our church and toilettes in Binga, the construction of the new houses in Nakangala, and exploring the new crops we wanted to introduce – Castor Beans and Cassava. Frank also took on the task of writing grants to various aid agencies for other projects we wanted to begin.

Slowly we realized the goals we had set for ourselves when we first came: to establish small Christian communities and create self-sustaining living conditions for the Tongas. Now, I combined my leadership training days with economic development training. Frank could break through the obstacles that tripped up the Tongas for years. He devoted his full atten-tion to these projects and others the Tongas identified. Frank and Hilde were still newlyweds when they arrived with us, and now they were an essential part of our team. Catechists and leaders from Nakangala and the new outstations we established often traveled to Binga to stay for a few days, and they too became more and more an essential part of the planning and development of the mission. Our original team of four continued to expand.

Chapter 23

Eastern Highlands February 1988

———————

In February 1988 Mary and some of the sisters in Bulawayo asked me to come with them on a ten-day silent retreat to the Eastern Highlands. They needed a priest to say Mass for them, and everyone felt comfortable with me joining them. I looked forward to the retreat, spending time with Mary and getting back to the beautiful mountains, the pine trees and the cool weather I experienced on our ten-day vacation there a year before.

Since October, when I returned from leave, Mary and I found more and more opportunities to spend time together. On my trips to Bulawayo, we always spent one day at Matopos and then made time to go to a nice restaurant where we would both dress up for a night out. Mary began to wear the jewelry I brought back from the States and would put on some perfume after we were out the door of the convent so as not to raise any suspicions.

We set off for the Eastern Highlands after Mass and breakfast one Wednesday morning. Sister Jacinta packed lunches for us all to eat on the way. I couldn't wait to see what kind of delicacies she made. Half of the sisters came with me in the Land Cruiser, and the other half went in a car.

Mary rode next to me in the front seat as she had on our vacation the year before. I felt myself relaxing as we left the cities behind and climbed into the piney forests and rushing streams of this part of the country, memories of our last vacation rising in my mind. We pulled into the long driveway that wound through the property and parked near the huge mansion where we would spend the next ten days in silence. I loved the Protea plants that dotted the landscape. They looked like huge colorful pinecones perched on the end of long stems, so different from anything I'd ever seen before. The smell of pine in the air and the mountain views reminded me a little of Switzerland which I visited a few times while I was a student in Rome.

The retreat director stayed in the room I occupied during our vacation the year before because it was private and large enough to meet with each of us for our individual sessions, so the sisters set up a bed for me in the dining room.

The first evening the retreat director explained to us the process of a silent retreat, "You will meet with me once a day to talk about anything you are experiencing. During that time I will give you scripture passages to reflect on. You can journal if you wish. The most important thing is silence. You are making this retreat together, but it is an individual experience. At some point, during the ten days, I will give you a break, an evening when we can relax and talk together but you are not to speak to anyone unless it is an emergency." She continued, "You don't have to stay in the house. Feel free to wander wherever you wish. But be here for meal times, Mass, and your appointment with me. Our retreat begins right now with evening prayer."

We all prayed together and finished singing a song and then went to bed. I looked forward to being in the mountains, resting, napping, hiking, and praying. I knew I couldn't talk to Mary, but I could enjoy looking at her.

I met with the retreat director the first morning around 11:00, and we talked for about thirty minutes about my expectations for the next ten days. Then she gave me my first exercise of the retreat. She told me to spend time trying to imagine my birth and the first few months or so of life in as much detail as I could.

"Picture yourself as a baby with your parents. Try to enter the scene as fully as you can, in as much detail as you can. Spend time with yourself as a small baby and see what happens."

I had never received this kind of assignment from a retreat director. I walked a few hundred yards from the house, climbed on top of a pile of boulders which shielded me from the others and sat down to enjoy a beautiful view of the mountains. I settled down there breathing slowly and closing my eyes, trying to bring to mind that scene of myself as a baby. I knew my parents lived in a tiny one-bedroom apartment in Toledo. My mother had told me I had colic as a baby. I saw myself suffering alone in the crib, crying and coughing, and I saw my parents standing over me, helpless in trying to comfort me. This image was so vivid and touched me so deeply that I sat on that rock for a long time. The feelings of loneliness and helplessness were so intense that I felt swept up in the experience as if I was living it at that moment. I was very familiar with isolation, but I never acknowledged the feeling of helplessness I now felt so intensely.

This image of myself was so startling that I felt drawn back to it every time I stopped to meditate in the course of the day and these feelings of loneliness and helplessness accompanied me until I fell asleep at night. I began to feel like I was falling slowly into a dark and bottomless pit. The next morning, I woke early and went for a walk, drawn to the same boulders I'd sat on the day before and found the image of this helpless baby still sharp and clear. By 11:00 that morning I felt exhausted. I reported my experience to the retreat director.

"Stay with this image, Mike, for another day. It is so intense and vivid for you. See what it has to teach you." I did not want to hear this. I hoped she'd give me some new assignment - a little relief. But instead of relief, she asked me to face those distressing images head on. I did feel lonely in the priesthood and helpless to change a life situation that seemed dire. As the days of the retreat went on it felt as if my entire ego was beginning to unravel, and I thought I was losing whatever sense of self I had so carefully constructed. I felt shocked at how quickly this "person" began to crumble. Suddenly I didn't know who I was and began to fear I was going insane. I felt isolated from the others, but the sense of isolation comforted me as well as terrified me. At that moment I couldn't relate to anyone. I felt sucked down into the experience. I couldn't talk about it. I didn't know where it was leading me. I felt completely lost.

During the day I spent time wandering around the hills and mountains, sitting on rock ledges or walking deep into the pine forest, alone. I needed to be away from people. I avoided any contact with the others, even Mary, and found eating meals with them challenging. I felt frightened because I didn't know how to find my way out of this feeling of deep despair. The only place I found solace was in the forest, where each afternoon I laid down on a soft carpet of pine needles and stared up at the tall trees as they swayed in the afternoon breeze. Breathing in the fragrant air, I let myself drift off to sleep, wake up, then go off to sleep again for hours. No one came looking for me, and I felt safe there alone.

Those months of daily journaling had prepared me for this experience. The journal afforded me the freedom to explore my deepest thoughts and desires without any filter or censorship. I exposed in that writing those feelings I had avoided and repressed for so long; my deep unhappiness, the sense that I was losing out on life. A few months earlier I journaled about an image that came to mind. I lay in a casket at the end of my life.

My dead-self looked straight at me and said, "Here lies a wasted life."

Here in the silence of this retreat in the mountains, I wondered, am I wasting my life? I saw this baby laying in a crib in the first few months of life. Then there I was lying in a casket at the end of my life. I faced an impossible choice: stay faithful to the commitment and the vows I took ten years earlier and live a life that looked lonely and joyless. Or I could break all my promises to start a new life with Mary which would mean disappointing family, friends, and even the Pope! The bridge to life with Mary seemed impossible to cross. The path I chose as a priest seemed impossible to live. There was no way out. A simple retreat exercise exposed the fragile structure of my life. For so long, I had let others determine the direction of my life, but now I saw that those I expected to save me were helpless too. For the first time, I saw that no one was going to come to "save" me because no one was able to do it for me. I felt vulnerable, overwhelmed, afraid, and alone. I regarded myself as a helpless baby, and I wept.

Day after day the isolation and feelings of darkness grew as I stayed with the image. I felt as if I were drowning, going deeper and deeper into the darkness. Even when the retreat director scheduled an evening of talking as a break from the silence of the retreat for everyone, I found it difficult to enter into the fun of the conversation.

The director recognized my deep distress and suggested that I listen to music to help me deal with it. She gave me a cassette with the soundtrack from Les Miserables.

Later, I returned the tape to her and told her, "I feel miserable enough already."

She decided to meet with me two times a day to monitor my progression or regression. I would have tried to steal some time with Mary, but I felt drained of any energy and found contact with anyone except the retreat director painful. For eight days I endured a darkness like I'd never experienced before and I worried I would never pull out of it. One evening I met with the retreat director for the second time that day. I continued to talk about the baby in the bassinet and myself in the casket.

She looked at me and said, "Mike, you are neither helpless nor dead. You are a 35-year-old man who has the power to choose your path. You can make a choice right now to keep staring at the darkness outside, or you can shift your gaze slightly and look to the light within you. The darkness will continue to pull you down. The light will free you."

I repeated what she told me, "Look to the light." I felt a little better, a little relief. "Look to the light," I said it again. "I think I feel better, freer," I told her. It was too simple, too easy. "Let me try this tonight and tomorrow." I left her room, got my jacket, and walked out into the cold night air. I walked up and down the long driveway that edged the property out to the road. I repeated the phrase over and over again, "Look to the light." Each time I said it I felt myself lifting a bit more until I felt more light than dark. I felt a new power flow through me by saying those words. It was up to me. I did not need to depend on a spiritual director, a discernment team, my friends, or anyone else to tell me what to do or to give me direction. I had to make a choice. It was that simple. What did I want to experience? The darkness? Or the light? It felt like a miracle. It had taken 16 years of conflicted feelings and this eight days of misery to come to that realization after 35 years of life. Whatever path I wanted to follow was my choice.

Over the next few days, I felt life coming back into me. I felt an inner strength and peace that came only by shifting my gaze and "looking to the light." I experienced a new power within me that would take decades to understand.

During the retreat, Mary and I knew that we would not be able to spend any time alone together, so we'd made a secret plan to stay in Harare for a few days afterward. This time, we didn't stay at a convent, we stayed in a little garden hotel and spent time walking in the city, in the parks, shopping, and eating at small cafes. By now we were deeply in love. For a brief time, we experienced what it was like to be a couple. One evening, we splurged and dined at a restaurant in the Monomatapa Hotel. I wore a shirt and tie, and Mary wore a white blouse, long red skirt, the red scarf I'd brought her in Toledo and a perfume I loved that had a light, fruity fragrance. When we arrived at the door of the restaurant, we read a sign that said, "Jacket and Tie Required." I had the tie but no jacket. When we told the waiter about this dilemma, he said that was no problem as they kept spares in a closet for just such an emergency. The only jacket I could find was two sizes too small for me. I walked into the restaurant feeling like a gorilla with my arms sticking out of the sleeves and the jacket gaping open in the front. We laughed and laughed about my elegant attire throughout the whole meal. Mary was my best friend, and I wanted to be with her all the time. But the wall of our vows towered between which we were afraid to tear down. We spent time talking about the future and how eventually each of us would be transferred by our superiors from Zimbabwe. I would go back to Toledo to work in a parish, and she might go anywhere in the world. Leaving the priesthood or the convent because we wanted to be together forever seemed out of the question. We had taken vows to sacrifice our lives for God regardless of whether we felt joy or happiness. I told myself that I had to be satisfied with that, but the frustration was becoming unbearable. The image of the casket with the words "wasted life" still haunted me.

Mary was scheduled to go on leave to Australia for three months beginning the end of September, and the thought of her leave affected me deeply. We planned to meet in Perth for two weeks on her way back to Zimbabwe. The weeks there would give us a chance to spend time together in a place where no one knew us, giving us the freedom we both desired.

Just before Mary went on leave, we planned another opportunity to spend a few days together. She had a few days off in August, and we arranged to meet at the Safari Lodge in Dette, half way between Bulawayo and Hwange and only a few hours from Binga. She hitched a ride with some of the sisters who were headed to Hwange for the weekend and told them she was meeting some friends at the lodge for a few days. After the sisters had dropped her off, I picked her up, and we drove out to the game reserve. I had booked a two-bedroom cabin for two nights. The cabin had a living room, a dining room, a front porch with chairs, a kitchen and the roof was a thick grass thatch. Mary had never stayed in a grass thatched cottage before which she found charming and romantic. We spent time driving into the game reserve looking at the giraffe, elephants, and warthogs. One evening we sat alone in one of the viewing platforms watching the animals. A pair of giraffes approached a small watering hole, and after drinking, we watched in amazement as the two began to entwine their long necks together in what seemed to us a mating ritual.

"I think those two are necking," Mary said.

We both thought that was the funniest thing we'd ever heard. In the evenings we would cook big meals together and sit outside on our porch watching the sunset over the savannah. The few days we spent together flew by, and within a few weeks, Mary was on her way to Australia.

We took bigger risks as we found more and more time to spend alone together, driven by passion on the one hand and held back by the promises we made on the other. This flood of emotion pounded against our solemn vows as we moved deeper into its current.

Chapter 24

Building Churches and Communities
November 1988

W hile I counted down the days until my departure for Perth, back
in Binga, the new All Souls Mission Church was under construction. The Church would have a nave with benches for the congregation, a
sanctuary for the altar and two back rooms; one for storage and one to keep
the robes and vestments for Mass. After three and a half years, we looked
forward to no longer having Mass in a tiny schoolroom.

Mike and Jules always wanted us to host the Tonga Musician's
Conference in Binga. As we made plans for the church, they insisted
that we make the building big enough to accommodate the crowds they
expected for the annual three-day conference. Mike and Jules worked with
Frank and the builders to secure the land to build and to help determine
how many outhouses we would need. It would not be unusual for hundreds
of people to attend such a conference where new music was presented and
learned. Despite how simple people's everyday lives were, their language
and music were very complex. Singing and dancing for hours or even all

night was something that everyone, young and old, men and women, participated in together.

By the end of September, about 80 adults came to Mass in Binga every week. We began to use the partially completed church structure. With Frank's keen oversight our modern rondavels in Nakangala, which we painted white inside and out, were almost finished. We hoped to have the houses completed before the rainy season began in November. Then if the rains came, at least we could stay out in Nakangala among the people, instead of hunkered down in Binga for weeks on end. Even though the houses would not have electricity or running water, we could stay there quite comfortably for a few weeks at a time, since clean drinking water and a functioning outhouse were nearby. There was a beautiful view of the mountains that surrounded the area from those houses.

The requests increased from people asking us to come and start new Christian communities in their area. Three years before, we'd spent hours sitting under trees waiting for someone to show up. Now people were coming to us as we visited outstations or dropped by our homes in Binga to request that we visit them. The first few years I lamented the lack of work and the weeks I spent sitting with nothing to do. Now we could hardly keep up with the demand not only to open new communities but also to start development projects we hoped would bring the Tonga people to some level of self-sufficiency. Some of the people who lived near the lake had begun a fishing cooperative. Other groups planned to start small businesses like a grinding mill, where people would bring their corn or millet seeds which saved the women the hours and hours it took to pound the grain with a large mortar and pestle.

One of the international aid agencies that worked in our area approached us to help them distribute donkeys to farmers so that people could plow their fields with an animal instead of hand hoeing. Hand hoeing had worked well when the Tongas were growing vegetables in small gardens along the Zambezi, but with the damming of the river to form Lake

Kariba, and the resettlement of the people onto this arid land, hand hoeing acres of corn or millet was back-breaking. Our little mission, among the poorest in this country, became a vibrant center for both religious and economic development.

It had been almost a year since I began writing my Tonga catechism and now it was ready to take to the printer for publishing. I couldn't wait to use it with all of our new little communities.

On November 13, 1988, we dedicated the church building in Binga. The week before the dedication there were still heaps of dirt and debris everywhere. But from Wednesday through Saturday night, dozens of people came, and we worked together raking, sweeping, polishing, digging and getting the place ready. On dedication day, it all looked spotless. A local Member of Parliament, the Provincial Administrator, all the local dignitaries, and Bishop Prieto from Hwange attended the dedication along with over a hundred local people. We started with a procession from the Primary School where we celebrated Mass for the past three years. We walked through the compound to the church where the Chief met us and said a prayer invoking all the spirits of the ancestors to be present and to bless us. Then we incensed the building while the whole community marched around singing. A big red ribbon stretched across the doorway which Bishop Prieto cut. Then we all entered the church for the first time.

During Mass, we celebrated the Confirmation of young people who wanted to take their faith to the next level, first Communion for many children, and the initiation of those who wanted to begin to study to become Catholic. At the end of Mass, I gave a speech – a brief history of the Church in Binga. At one point I mentioned that a young priest – Fr. Ignatius Prieto, the current Bishop, who was among the first priests in Binga. The whole congregation jumped to their feet clapping and ululating. Then each person I named in my little history stood and was acknowledged. It was great fun to give a history where most of the founders were still alive and present.

After Mass, the women served nsima for everyone. The mission provided beef which most people only got to eat during big celebrations like this one. The rest of the day people stayed at our new church eating, singing, and dancing. The drummers had endless energy and kept the celebration going late into the night.

With the opening of new places to visit, the dedication of two churches, building two new houses in Nakangala, Jules's women's groups, Frank's development work, and Julitta's work in Kamitivi, Mike and I would occasionally look at each other and say, "Wow! We have a real mission." Gone were the days of waiting around for something to happen. Things were finding us, and we felt excited, invigorated, and exhausted.

I was ready for a break and looked forward to spending two weeks with Mary in Perth. As the time grew nearer, so did my excitement and anticipation.

(Photo: Nakangala Church being built)

Chapter 25

Perth December 1988

A few days before my flight left from Harare to Perth, Mike and Jules drove me from Binga to Victoria Falls where I boarded a flight to Harare. I spent the next day walking around in a blissful daze, thinking about spending the next two weeks alone with Mary.

That evening I stood on the steps of the Meikles hotel waiting for the airport shuttle bus. It was hot and muggy in Harare. Wreaths and lights hung from the palm trees decorated the streets. After four years it still felt odd to be wearing shorts at Christmastime. I felt anxious about getting to the airport on time and then relief when the bus pulled into the circular drive in front of the hotel. The driver stowed our bags, we all found our seats, and he pulled out of the drive and into traffic. I let out a sigh and felt my whole body relax. I was on my way. It had been a three-day journey from the dusty bush of Binga, to the beauty of Victoria Falls, to the hustle and bustle of the city of Harare, and now in a few more miles, I'd be at the airport where I would board the plane for Perth, and Mary.

I looked out the window as we passed out of the city and everything looked fantastic. I could see the ladies with their colorful wraps and headdresses selling crafts, the flowering bougainvillea lining the road, and the exotic tropical birds flitting from branch to branch. I looked out and took it all in, not wanting to miss this moment of happiness and relief. I could see the fields of corn and wheat, the red roof tiles of the city homes and the thick grass thatch of the village rondavels from the bus window. The trees shimmered in the evening light as the sun sank lower on the horizon. Everything shimmered. I breathed deeply and let out another sigh releasing worry and stress, years of it, maybe decades. Everyone on the bus seemed to be smiling. I took it all in, each moment, as the bus picked up speed on the highway toward the airport. Could everyone see how happy I felt? I smiled at everyone who looked my way.

"Where are you going?" the woman sitting next to me asked.

"I'm going to Perth."

"Oh, my! That is a long, long journey," she said.

I asked her the same question.

"Going to Vic Falls," she said.

We chatted the rest of the way. It all felt great.

We rolled into the airport, and I gave the driver a few dollars as he handed me my bags. A long line of people stood waiting to pass through security. It didn't matter. I had plenty of time. I couldn't believe I was going to Perth to be alone with Mary for two solid weeks. It took 30 minutes to get from the city center in Harare out to the airport, but it would be another nine hours before the plane touched down in Australia. As I sat at the gate, I thought about how this whole adventure in Zimbabwe began with Hoffman's simple question five years earlier: "Mike, have you ever thought about going to Africa?"

Once we took off, I sat staring at the big screen in the front of the flight cabin that showed our progress toward Australia. I watched as the plane left the coast of Africa and began to head out over the Pacific. Then I dozed off, and the next time I looked up, we were in the middle of the Pacific.

162

From that halfway point we seemed to inch along the flight path. The economy seats didn't accommodate my 6'3" frame, and I found it difficult to go back to sleep. My pounding heart didn't help either. Eight hours into the flight we approached the coast of Australia, and Perth showed up bigger on the screen. And as the plane descended, I saw the port with large container ships and sailboats. Then we flew over houses in neat little neighborhoods like I'd seen when I lived in Liverpool, England one summer. Finally, we flew over the city buildings of Perth. I was back in a first-world country, and it felt like home. What would Mary be wearing? What if she changed her mind about us while she visited her family at home? Mary left for home four months earlier, and I had missed seeing her so much. A little worry crept into my mind. Maybe this wasn't such a good idea? But I was already there; the plane touched down and rolled up to the gate.

The walk to immigration and customs seemed endless, and there were hundreds and hundreds of people walking with me. Where did they all appear? We wound our way through the barriers like we were standing in line for a ride at an amusement park. I felt more and more anxious and excited about seeing Mary. I got my passport stamped and then waited at the carousel for my bags. I could see the terminal and all the people standing out there, but I couldn't see Mary. The carousel revolved endlessly, and I began to worry that something happened to my bags. My bags appeared, and I grabbed them and walked to customs.

"Nothing to declare," I said, and the officer waved me through.

I made my way out into the terminal. I was actually in Australia. Walking out into the bright terminal from the dark baggage and customs area I was a little blinded by the light. Where was she? I stood there looking, searching the crowd. Then I felt a tap on my shoulder, and as I turned, I felt her arms around my neck and her lips on mine.

"Darling, you made it. I missed you so much," she said.

She hadn't changed her mind about us after all. All my worries vanished as she kissed me again.

"I love your haircut," I said.

"I told the hairdresser I needed a unique cut because I was meeting people in Perth."

Her hair was very short on the sides with loads of curls on top. She wore white pants, a pink blouse, and sandals. I noticed just a hint of perfume. It was the same scent she wore just before she left when we were in Harare, a light fragrance I loved. She smelled delicious! "You look and smell great," I told her. I couldn't take my eyes off her.

"We better not stand here all day. Let's get the shuttle into the city," she said.

On the bus ride into Perth, Mary said, "The hotel is fantastic. Our room has a beautiful view of the river. It's right in the middle of the city. I can't wait until you see it."

Mary had arrived from Melbourne the evening before. The bus ride took thirty minutes, and we talked the whole way. The bus dropped us right in front of the Esplanade Hotel. It looked like an apartment building to me. The main lobby was all tile floors, no carpeting with black chairs scattered all around. Mary took me straight to the elevator. I just hoped the room looked a little cozier. We walked down the dark hallway and Mary opened the door to our room and light flooded in from the window. I walked over to see a beautiful panorama of the Swan River. There were palm trees dotted along the shore and sailboats in the bay. Our room had a king bed, carpeting on the floor, and a small round table with two chairs. Mary came up behind me and put her arms around me again. We were finally alone with two glorious weeks without any worries or cares.

We spent the rest of the afternoon in the room, enjoying the view from the window, napping, and feeling the glorious freedom of being together. For the first time, we allowed ourselves to express the deep passionate love we felt for one another. In the early evening, we walked around the city, ate seafood in a little restaurant and then walked around the city some more enjoying one another's company and this new intoxicating freedom. Here in Perth, we were breaking almost every rule, but compelled by such a deep passion and love that we had denied ourselves it didn't feel wrong. We let ourselves experience life in a new way for the first time without inhibition or prohibition. It felt magnificent! Every moment sparkled.

We went out into the city the next day to find Perth crowded with Christmas shoppers. We walked hand in hand through the crush of people out on Saturday shopping sprees. Half the time I didn't know where I was. I was just happy and content to be with Mary. Later we walked along the Swan River and into some of the neighborhoods. We stumbled on a Pizza Hut, and I convinced Mary that she had to try an American style pizza. We ate a pepperoni pizza and drank Australian beer. It didn't matter what we did because here we were a couple. In the evening we went to Mass at St. Mary's Cathedral. It stood in green space in the center of Perth. We sat toward the back and felt so small in the midst of the towering granite arches and the rose marble floors. The cathedral glimmered in the evening light. It felt good to be sitting there with Mary and not up front running the show as the celebrant of the Mass. I felt even closer to God from the pews. I loved being a couple with her.

Geraldton

On Sunday, we took a bus out to the airport where we rented a little Ford Fiesta and drove north to the seaside resort town of Geraldton. The roads were empty that Sunday morning, and before long we were out of Perth and into the glorious desolation of Western Australia. Over the course of the next 250 miles, we drove through countryside that reminded me of the open savannah of Zimbabwe and then through small towns that reminded me of the picturesque villages I'd seen when I lived in England. But no matter where we drove, everything shimmered because we were together.

We arrived in Geraldton at about 4:00 in the afternoon, found the condo I had rented and checked in. It had one bedroom, a combination kitchen, dining room, and living room, and a large bathroom with shower. It was a five-minute walk to the beach and a ten-minute drive to town.

We established a routine of going to town each morning to buy our food for the day; we called it "going marketing." Geraldton sat on the coast and had a significant population of Western Australia, so we had easy access to plenty of grocery stores and fresh fish markets. Most of our meals featured seafood of some kind. Shopping for food together for the first time became an adventure for us. We thought of a grocery store as a treasure house where we could buy whatever we wanted. We felt a delicious selfishness which neither of us had ever experienced before, and rather than trying to analyze the right or wrong of it all we decided to "live fully" each moment since we did not know if there would ever be a chance like this again. Everything seemed new and beautiful and glorious and illicit.

In the afternoon, we would take off to see some sight in the area. We visited a recreated 1800's town that had a jail that imprisoned aboriginal people who had broken the law. The guide told us that many died there because they could no longer see the sky. My new found freedom was so exhilarating that this story touched me. Had I locked myself up for all of these years? Had I imprisoned myself by failing to follow my own heart's desire? I felt deeply what those aboriginal people must have felt as they sat locked in a small, dank cell cut off from nature and the world around them.

Around 3:00 in the afternoon we would walk to the beach and spend the rest of the day swimming, dozing, and chatting. The days flowed in this gentle rhythm. In the evening, Mary would cook a gourmet supper for us. And then we'd walk on the beach under the brilliant night sky of the Southern Hemisphere, read for a while, and then go to sleep.

There seemed to be endless things to talk about and share. We loved the freedom of our physical intimacy, but we were careful in how far we would go. Our feelings for one another by now were explosive, and it became harder and harder not to express those emotions completely. We felt we had put enough limits on ourselves to be safe. There was one moment of intimacy where I worried that I had perhaps gone a bit too far. I resolved to be more careful in the future as I didn't want to put myself or Mary in a compromising position. We had already compromised our moral standards and our vows enough. It all felt right. The flow of emotion and passion carried us into deeper that expressions of our love for each other.

The week in Geraldton soon came to an end. We packed up and moved to our next destination; Busselton, Western Australia.

Busselton

It took us two days to make the journey from Geraldton to Busselton on the southern tip of Western Australia. On the way, we stopped at a beautiful old Inn in New Norcia that preserved the best of late-1800's architecture. The Inn had a wide veranda that stretched across the entire front of the building. Inside the front entrance stood a large lobby and a wide winding staircase that lead to the second floor and the bedrooms. An enormous four-poster bed, antique chairs, and a balcony with two cafe chairs and a small round table completed our room. After we had unpacked, we went down to the pub on the ground level. We heard the sound of laughter and shouting first, and when we walked in, we found the place jam packed with guests and locals. The barmaid showed us to a booth. I wasn't sure what do next.

"Go up to the bar and order us some drinks," Mary said.

"What do I order? I'll sound odd to them. Why don't you go up?" I said.

"That will look strange. Men do the ordering in a pub here. Just go up there and order something."

I slid out of the booth and pushed my way to the bar. "I'd like a glass of white wine and a pint of beer please."

"Hey everyone, we got a Yank here," the bartender shouted to the guys at the bar. "Help him pick a beer for himself and wine for his Sheila." Everyone immediately came over, slapped me on the back, and helped me make my choices. When I got back to the booth, I said, "Everyone thinks your name is Sheila."

"That's what people here call a girl, stupid." And she laughed and laughed about that.

We soaked up the good-humored atmosphere as well as the peaceful presence we felt in one another's company. There was no need or pressure to be anything different.

The next morning, we stopped first into a Benedictine Monastery that was filled with aboriginal religious art, from the stained glass windows to the statues of saints and then drove to a deserted beach where we spent a few hours swimming and relaxing in the sea. In the afternoon we found a huge state park called The Pinnacles, a place filled with rocky projections that looked like missiles ready for launch. We discovered the wonders of Western Australia as we discovered the wonders of being together. I couldn't stop looking at her.

Late in the afternoon, we passed through Bunbury and arrived at Busselton where we had reserved a cottage for our second week. It turned out to be an "A-frame" chalet set back a bit from the beach. The first floor had a kitchen, dining room, and living room that opened onto a wide front porch. The second floor was a bedroom loft that looked down into the living room and out through an enormous front window to the sea. We resettled into our established routine; marketing in the morning, a tour in the late morning or early afternoon, beach time in the late afternoon, a big dinner, walk under the stars and then bed. Time flowed from one moment to the next.

One day we drove through a Kerri Tree Forest. These magnificent trees had white trunks and grew over 200 feet tall. When we stopped to get out of the car, everything was silent except for the wind and the birds. There was a hazy light that filled the forest with an enchanted look.

We followed signs to a tree that had a fire tower platform in its canopy. Mary thought climbing to the top would be fun. When we arrived at the small parking lot, we found a few cars under the great tree that stood before us. I should have realized what I was getting into when I read the sign, "Climbing Certificates Available at the Office." Why would anyone need or even want a climbing certificate? Then I looked up. This Kerri tree must have been 250 feet tall and 15 feet around. I could just make out a viewing platform near the very top. But to reach the platform we had to climb a winding ladder-like structure created by driving huge metal stakes into the tree's trunk every foot or so. There was no safety rail except for a barrier of thin wire wrapped around the outside of the stakes. As I was considering an alternative option, Mary had already started climbing. "What are you waiting for?" She said.

I looked up, and she disappeared around the back of the tree. Here we go again, I thought. Images of that mountain we climbed in the Eastern Highlands flooded my mind. As I climbed higher and higher, I held onto the tree to brace myself. I became more frightened the higher up I went and hoped that I wouldn't slip and fall through the bars. The picture of my lifeless form stretched out on the ground below rose like a haunting specter. Even more distressing, people were climbing down these steps at the same time. So at points on the way, someone had to press against the tree to let people coming down pass by stepping on the outer edge.

As I climbed higher, and higher I could feel my muscles tense. Ahead of me, Mary seemed to be gliding toward the top, greeting every passerby, while I inched my way painfully up the tree. By now Mary had moved yards ahead of me scampering up the stairs like a monkey. "Hey, maybe we should turn around and go back down. It feels a little wobbly to me" I said to her.

(Photo: The Tree)

"You can do what you like," she said, "I am going up to the top."

She disappeared again around the huge trunk moving faster than before. I couldn't see her. I couldn't see the top. And I was afraid to look down. Climbing higher and higher I felt less and less secure, and so I grabbed each bar tighter and tighter. Mary seemed to have the nerves of a tightrope walker. "One false step and I will be a squashed bug," I groaned just loud enough for the people coming down the tree to hear. Did they just move around me a little faster? People descending the steps looked at me with pity. Finally, I pulled myself into the very top canopy and walked onto the platform in the upper part of the tree. The view of the forest and the surrounding countryside was stunning. However, I could barely move because my muscles had tensed up so badly as I clung for dear life to each rung of the passage. We spent a good deal of time at the top holding one another and looking out over this beautiful Kerri tree forest. When it looked like the way down was clear we began our descent.

I noticed that people either went down face first or butt first. Face first meant looking straight down the 250-foot drop; straight into the jaws of death. I chose to go down the "baby way." Mary glided down the stairway, reaching the bottom way before I crawled off the last rung. I could have kissed the ground, utterly grateful to be standing on earth. Afterward, we took each other's picture clinging to the steps of the tree. I tried to put on a brave face, but I wanted to put as much distance as I could between me and that monster. I was discovering that Mary had an inner strength and ability to face any challenge, whether it was climbing a mountain or scaling a tree. And while she loved me and treasured our moments together, she possessed an independent spirit that invited me to come along with her but did not demand anything beyond what I was willing to give. Now I felt both love and admiration for her. And I thought, maybe we'd be able to figure out a future together after all.

The next day we drove to the southwestern most tip of Australia, where the Indian and the Pacific oceans meet. On the way back we stopped into a Catholic church that had beautiful views of the sea. The altar and all of the furniture were carved from Kerri Trees.

In the evening, we walked on the beach and looked at the lights of Bunbury down the shore and the beautiful bright stars above and listening to the rolling waves of the ocean. It gave us a deep sense of serenity, peace, and togetherness. We stood there holding hands and looking out to the sea and up to the heavens, and we felt a sense of oneness that we couldn't express in words. Mary talked about her family in Nathalia, Victoria and I spoke about my family in Toledo, Ohio. It felt normal to be talking more about family and less about ministry. We were both becoming aware that this magical time together was winding down. The exuberance we had felt at the airport in Perth gave way to the dim realization that in a few days we would be headed for Africa and our "real lives," apart from one another for months and eventually years at a time. Neither of us felt ready to talk about that yet, the magic of our togetherness was too strong. I wanted some outside force to intervene somehow to save me from what felt like my fate, but at the same time, I could hear the words of my retreat director: "Look to the light within you. You can choose." But I didn't know how.

We spent less time on the beach in this week and more time touring the area. This area was rolling and misty, with roads that wound through the hills and in and out of the forests.

As we drove out of a small town where we'd filled the car with gas, Mary looked at me and asked, "Have you felt sick at all lately? I wonder if I ate something that didn't agree with me."

"Not really. The road has been curvy, and occasionally I get a little queasy but not sick." I said.

"Well, I feel a little sick right now, and there aren't any curves in this road," she said.

I told her to wait and see how she felt later, maybe she needed an aspirin.

The Kerri Forest kept calling us back. We loved to drive through it and walk among those towering ancient trees. It was a magical place that mirrored the enchanted feeling I was experiencing. As each day passed the topic of our return arose more often, and the reality of our situation replaced the magic we had felt before. Here there was uninterrupted time together. There we had snatches of time, moments together that we stole every few months. I projected into the future when Mary returned to England or some other country, and I to Ohio. We might see one another every few years if we were lucky. These thoughts were so painful that I couldn't bear to express them, let alone think about them for long and I focused my attention on the few remaining days left.

Perth

As our week ended, we drove back to Perth. At the end of our journey, we rented an efficiency apartment in the center of the city. We walked through a back alley, then along a passageway that seemed more like a factory entrance and then into an apartment. Our Camelot was fading. Once we were back in Zimbabwe, there was no guarantee when we might see one another again. So we decided to celebrate our own private Christmas.

The next morning, we both went Christmas shopping. The present I wanted to give her came from a jeweler. We spent the whole morning shopping for each other, and we met at a coffee shop in the middle of Perth when we finished. Then we bought our Christmas dinner to cook back at the apartment. Mary insisted on cooking the entire dinner herself.

"I want the whole kitchen to myself, so I'm not banging into you all the time," she said.

I happily sipped a beer and watched her cook.

"Stop staring at me," she said, "it's a little freaky."

"I can't help it," I asked her to bring me another beer but got a towel in the face from the kitchen instead.

"Get up and get your beer. I'm busy cooking for you."

We sat down to a roast beef dinner complete with potatoes and carrots and Yorkshire pudding. We bought a Christmas pudding to share including rum sauce. After we had eaten, we exchanged presents.

"I want to give you something special that will remind you of Australia and also that will remind you of me," I said, and handed her a small box, wrapped in Christmas paper by the jeweler. She opened it to find an opal ring. "Here, let me put it on your finger." I slipped it on her finger, and it felt like a proposal. She loved it. Opals are the Australian gem.

"I can't believe you would give me something so beautiful," she said. She kept holding it up to the light and showing me how it would make the opal in the ring change colors. Every once in a while I would catch her looking at her hand. The next evening, we went to a lovely restaurant for dinner in a park overlooking the city and Mary wore her ring. Mary wore a long flowing skirt, a white blouse, and a broad red belt. I wore a gray blazer over my blue shirt and gray slacks. We wanted to dress up a little. After our meal, we walked to the park and stood quietly at an overlook admiring the city, the Swan River, and the Sea. We asked another couple passing by to take our picture. We stood quietly, holding hands. Time was moving faster now toward the end, and while we both wanted to stay and continue experiencing the depth of our love, we knew it couldn't last.

As we held one another, Mary whispered to me, "You've touched my very soul."

I felt my heart break open and didn't want to let her go.

We spent the next morning packing and then in the evening dressed up and went to the fanciest restaurant I had ever eaten at, Ruby's. We enjoyed champagne sorbet between every course to clear the palate. Next to us sat a couple who enjoyed the sorbet and each other in between courses. Mary kept pointing out the way the guy would "move in" on his girlfriend.

"Australian guys are very smooth at this," she told me. Then she would accurately predict his next move.

This couple provided our personal floor show.

"You must have had some pretty good experiences of this in your past I need to know about," I said. Mary looked at me out of the corner of her eye and winked. But this interlude of happiness was coming to an end.

Back to Harare

The next morning, we drove to the airport and dropped off the car. Back to reality. I felt terrible, the way I felt walking out of church on my ordination day and being greeted by my old girlfriend. It felt like my biggest mistake yet. As we waited for the plane, Mary's name came over the loudspeaker, and she walked to the ticket counter where the agent told her she could move to first class. She asked if there was room for me too. The agent reluctantly found me a seat. However, when we boarded the 747, I felt a wave of despair as Mary went to her place on the top area and I found my seat on the bottom. So instead of having 9 hours to talk about what we experienced and what would we do next, we had to fly the whole way apart. The feeling of gloom and doom overwhelmed me. By the time we reached Harare, I was an emotional mess. Luckily, Mary's flight to Bulawayo was delayed, and my flight to Victoria Falls didn't leave until the next day. We had one more night together. But the magic spell was broken. We were both exhausted from the flight and so went to bed and the next day went our separate ways. It would be months before we would see one another again.

Chapter 26

Christmas in Binga December 1988

———

Both Jules and Mike came to meet me when I arrived in Vic Falls the next day. They could see my state of emotional shutdown, so we stopped at the Baobab Hotel in Hwange to fortify ourselves with Carlton Beer and a big basket of chicken and chips. They asked me about the trip to Perth and Mary. We talked for quite a while about the things I'd seen and done. Later I would talk to Mike in more detail, sitting in our usual spot out under the stars behind our houses in Binga. Everything had seemed so fantastic and looked so shimmering just a few weeks ago with my trip ahead of me. Now with the journey behind me, the darkness crept back in and surrounded me.

I told Mike, "I feel trapped again like I am letting another chance at happiness just slip through my fingers." He listened. " I know that if I asked Mary to leave, she would do it. But I just don't know how. I guess I need a miracle." There wasn't an easy answer I could think of to resolve this dilemma.

Back in Binga Jules, Mike, and I got ready for the Christmas season. In the two weeks leading up to Christmas, we visited all of our stations while the weather stayed dry so that we could have Christmas Mass celebrations with everyone. Mike and I visited 15 outstations on a regular basis. The rains held off long enough for us to make it everywhere, and slowly I settled back into life in Binga.

We invited all of our ex-patriot friends to our gazebo for a feast on Christmas Day. We bought a sheep and Mike and I grilled it on the big brick barbecue pit we built right next to the gazebo. We had a great time eating the mutton, drinking beer and singing Christmas carols from everyone's native country. It wasn't quite the same as the Christmas I experienced with Mary in Perth, but it did help to ease the pain of separation from her. After the party, Mike and I sat out in our chairs under the stars and talked long into the night. Just like old times! But now instead of the challenges of the team and the leadership, I talked about Mary, priesthood, and my vow of celibacy and Mike shared his struggles with priesthood and celibacy. Our conversations deepened with each passing night, and slowly I felt myself opening up to Mike more and more, finally facing what I felt. Until Mike arrived in Binga, I had kept all of this bottled up, unspoken. Or if I did talk about this to another priest, it was dismissed as the common struggle and sacrifice required of my vocation, just like in college and theology. Mike asked me to tell him more and encouraged me to go deeper. I felt safe with him in exploring my feelings, fears, and deepest desires. It felt like I was continuing what had begun on the retreat a few months earlier, something within me was opening.

The rains came after Christmas. They were sporadic enough that we still made it out to the villages to visit, teach, pray for the sick, and have Mass. At a few of the outstations, people were getting ready for baptism and we wondered what to do with the men who had more than one wife. Sometimes the men took on the wife of a brother who had died to make sure she and her children had enough food, clothing, and shelter. At other times, another wife was taken because of a more romantic reason. But whatever the case, it was a problem we were not sure how to handle. A few of the communities began to make plans for a grinding mill and a fishing cooperative and so we visited them to see what progress they made and what we needed to do to keep the ball rolling. I still had a dream of planting a cashew grove but no one had bitten on that hook yet. There was also a European man who came out to our area and who wanted to introduce Cassava – a root crop, a little like growing potatoes, except that once planted a farmer only harvested what tubers were needed and left the rest to grow the next year again. It looked like nsima and was an excellent food source for other parts of drought-stricken Africa. But the people liked the taste of their corn meal, so the Cassava idea would have to wait.

I called and wrote to Mary every week.

(Photo: Mike and Mary in Perth)

Chapter 27

Breaking News February 10, 1989

———————

A t the beginning of February Julitta, Jules, Mike and I went to Bulawayo for a shopping trip and a few days out of the bush. Two months had passed since I left Mary in Harare. I looked forward to town life, electricity, and time alone with her.

The four of us got into our usual shopping routine; going to the warehouse store, filling the Land Rover with supplies and then eating lunch in a restaurant - usually for a hamburger and fries. In the evening Mary and I spent time together walking around the convent grounds. She was very concerned about her feelings of sickness and the discomfort she had in her abdomen. No matter what Mary tried, the pain seemed to be getting worse. She didn't know what was happening. We hadn't talked about this before, and it was the first time I knew about any problems. We talked about our moments of intimacy but wondered how anything could have happened since we had been so careful not to go too far. Mary had seen the doctor, and he scheduled a scan for her the next afternoon.

The next day Mike and I went into town for more supplies, and as we walked to the store, I confided to him that I felt worried about the whole situation with Mary. Mike didn't say anything, but his look communicated concern. Later that day Mary stopped in to see me in my room before she went to the doctor and told me she'd let me know what they found as soon as she returned. I sat alone in my room worrying about what she might find out. Around 4:00 there was a knock at my door. Mary didn't wait for me to say, "Come in."

She swept into my room, sat on my bed, took my hand, looked me in the eye and said, "I'm pregnant! I was laying on the scan table, and the technician was talking to me about what she was seeing. Then the technician said, 'And there is the baby.' I freaked out. I was so agitated that the technician had to call the doctor."

Mary told me that the doctor tried to calm her down by telling her that everything looked healthy and that he would take care of her. She looked at him and shouted, "It's all normal for anyone else. It's not normal for a nun!"

He said something about how uptight the Catholic church was and dismissed the whole thing as irrelevant. He was more concerned about Mary and the baby. It was February 10, 1989. We sat in total shock. Then Mary immediately left to tell the news to Sr. Eileen, her superior. I left to buy a big pack of cigarettes and a bottle of rum. Later, Mary came to talk to me again.

"Eileen was fantastic. She sat there and listened to me. She didn't judge or blame me at all," Mary said. "Tomorrow, Eileen wants to talk to both of us for a little while. But for now, she doesn't want us to say anything."

Evening prayers were about to begin, and we both rushed to the chapel so we wouldn't be late. The last thing we wanted to do was to raise any suspicion. We'd planned a dinner date that evening at our favorite French restaurant in Bulawayo, Che` Nic.

Once seated at our table, the waiter had brought us our bread basket I said, "Now that I am over the initial shock of your news I feel strangely happy about the whole situation. I feel so close to you now, connected in a deeper way than before." Mary looked at me. She was strong and vulnerable at the same time, and I fell in love with her all over again. "I need to take a little time to make sure that when I make this decision, it will be the right one."

"Take all the time you need," she said.

For a long time, I just looked into her eyes not speaking. I felt she was looking into <u>my</u> very soul now. Mary was going to have a baby in August - our baby!

After we had returned from dinner, we took a long walk and talked late into the night in my room. The next morning I had Mass for the sisters. After breakfast, Mary and I went to Sr. Eileen's office. Mary and I were both 36 years old, and Eileen was a few years older. We were all adults facing an unusual situation, and that's the way Sr. Eileen treated us. There was no recrimination, judgment, or blame. She was kind and understanding and oddly a little excited about the whole situation.

"So you're going to have a baby, you two," she said. I was more prepared for a tongue lashing than a baby shower. "How did you keep your cool during Mass today, Mike? I'm not sure I could have done that, not with the situation you are dealing with."

I had spent so much time pretending to be happy over the years that pretending that nothing was wrong came pretty easily.

"Ok. We're not going to say anything at all to anyone about this until we have a good plan in place," Sr. Eileen said. "First of all, we need to take care of Mary and the baby. I am going to make a few calls and see what I can arrange. In the meantime, you two better sort out your plans." Then she ended it all with, "A baby! Oh my!"

Our trip out to Matopos was different this time. We found a small pond in the park and decided to lay out a blanket here instead of climbing the rocks. We wanted to spend most of our time talking about what we were going to do next. We felt terribly embarrassed about the whole situation. We had always been the responsible ones, the ones in charge, the ones who took care of other people's mistakes. Now the tables were turned. Would anyone take care of us? Mary didn't have any choice. She was going to have a baby. I was amazed at how calm she seemed already, the same calm I'd seen when she was climbing mountains or scaling that monster tree.

"If you decide to leave and we get married, would you be willing to do anything to support us? You might have to sweep floors or something at first," she said.

I told her that sweeping floors and living with her forever sounded better to me than the way I lived for the past ten years. I still wanted to take a little time to make sure that this was the choice I wanted and not just because I had gotten myself "into a jam." Mary was patient and understanding, but the clock was ticking, and I knew I needed to make a decision.

Both of us couldn't believe that one moment of indiscretion, one moment when we had gotten a little too close could result in pregnancy. We rehashed our time in Perth over and over, trying to figure it out. It almost seemed like a virgin birth. Regardless of what we thought, the fact remained, Mary was pregnant. That evening I told Mike the news, and he looked at me with shock and empathy. I was not looking forward to telling my mother and father, my brothers and sister, the Bishop, and the hundreds and hundreds of parishioners in Toledo and in Liverpool who knew I was in Zimbabwe, and who had been tracking my progress and praying for me.

The fact that I had no source of income and no marketable skills, no home or furniture of my own was a huge problem. I was a long way from home in Toledo, and the baby was due in seven months. We decided to keep this a secret between us, Mike and Sr. Eileen until we were ready to make an announcement.

It was time to head back to Binga. Mary and I had a few moments together before I left.

"I will let you know as soon as I decide what I am going to do. I am going to spend some time in Harare talking to our retreat director to see if she can help me sort things out." We kissed goodbye. I climbed into the Land Rover with Mike and my other teammates and drove out of Bulawayo.

If I was an emotional mess coming back from Perth, I was out of my mind at this point. When we arrived in Binga, the rains began in earnest, and we couldn't get out at all. The roads were too dangerous. It rained almost continuously. We had never experienced this kind of tropical monsoon. Later that week I boarded a big green bus in Binga and rode it to Bulawayo. I sat looking out the window as the bus rumbled along remembering the first big green bus ride I took from Mutoko to Harare and the big green bus we took from Bulawayo after the crash. Now here was the bus taking me on another journey. I stayed a night in Bulawayo and saw Mary briefly and then took the coach from Bulawayo to Harare. In Harare, I stayed with our retreat director, Sr. Regina. I hoped she could help me sort things out the same way she had helped me "look to the light" on our retreat. Most of my days in Harare were spent wandering around the neighborhood where she lived. Eventually, I stumbled upon a cemetery and for some reason found it comforting. I felt the close presence of my Grandma Schoenhofer who had always been a strong silent presence in my childhood. She loved it when I would sit next to her when we visited. A peaceful and accepting aura surrounded her. I needed that atmosphere right now. I found grappling with my thoughts easier in the quiet of the cemetery, with my Grandma there to help me. But after five days I still felt confused. I took the coach back to Bulawayo and spent the night in a hotel. Mary came to visit me again.

I told her, "I am still working on it." And she smiled, but she seemed a bit more nervous now.

Back in Binga, the rains were relentless. For two weeks all I did was read novels and walk around the house in a stupor. In the meantime, the replacement vehicle for our Land Rover, which had been shaking apart for the past few months, arrived in Harare. Mike got sick of seeing me in this state of gloom.

"I want you to go to Harare tomorrow and wait until the new vehicle gets through customs. I don't care how long you stay there but don't come back to Binga until you've made a decision one way or the other."

I felt grateful for this clear directive. There was nothing happening in Binga anyway, and someone had to be in Harare. The next day I took the big green bus back to Bulawayo.

I got a room in the same hotel in downtown Bulawayo and stayed there for the weekend. Mary and I spent what time she could get away from the convent.

"Eileen has arranged for me to stay with her brother, who used to be a priest and his wife and family in Leeds, England while I wait for the baby to come," she said.

She and Sr. Eileen were moving forward with plans. I felt relieved that Mary was going to be staying with people who would understand our situation. It was one small step in the right direction.

"I am going to leave Zimbabwe in four weeks," she said.

Time was running out for me to make a decision.

Traveling to Harare on the same coach Marge and I had ridden in the first weeks when we arrived, I tried to imagine what kind of jobs I could get. Perhaps I could farm raspberries at a "U Pick It" orchard. I thought maybe I could be a writer. I wondered what I could do to support a wife and a child. Here was everything I dreamed about coming true, but not the way I'd planned. Maybe my request to the Universe wasn't specific enough: I wanted a family, I forgot to mention that I also needed a job and a home to go with it.

On this trip to Harare I arranged to stay with some Dominican sisters who lived in a house in the suburbs. While I waited for the car to move through customs, I wandered around the neighborhood and happened upon a park and another cemetery. On the weekend I went back to Bulawayo and checked into the same hotel. I asked Mary to come by that evening.

"Sit down here." I patted the place next to me on the bed. The room was small with only a bed and a straight back chair. She sat on the bed waiting for me to speak. "It's kind of weird. Both times I went to Harare I found a cemetery where I felt the close presence of my grandmother, my father's mother. This time she felt closer to me, and I felt a deep peacefulness come over me. I have come to a decision. I am going to leave the priesthood so we can be married."

Her whole body collapsed into me, and she sighed with deep relief. We hugged and held one another for a long time.

I had no idea how this was all going to unfold, and the road ahead seemed almost impossible to navigate. We decided to tell our families. Back in Harare, I asked the sisters for permission to call home. I felt so nervous about telling my mother and father "the news" that I wrote out what I planned to say.

I waited for a time when the sisters were gone and then dialed my parent's number in Toledo, hoping they were home. After a few rings, I heard my mother's voice, "Hello."

"Hello Mom, it's me."

"Well this is a surprise," she said. I heard her say, "Bill, it's Mickey on the phone."

Then I said, "Mom, I have something important to tell you and dad, but I am so nervous that I had to write it out. I'm going to read it to you and then when I've finished we can talk about it. Ok?"

There was silence on the other end of the phone, and finally, mom said, "OK, go ahead."

Then I told them the story of Perth that Mary was pregnant, and that I planned to leave the priesthood so we could be married. I said we planned to live in America. There was silence again.

After some time, Mom said, "That is pretty shocking news."

We talked for a bit, and then I said, "Would you call the others (my brothers and sister)?"

Mom agreed and then she asked, "When is Mary due?"

"She's due in August, Mom," I said. "I know this has been a big shock for you. It's a big shock for me too. I'll call you back in a few days. Ok?"

"That's fine," Mom said, "We love you."

"I love you too." And then we hung up. I started to cry. I felt relieved that I had gotten the news out and regretful about the deep hurt and disappointment that I was causing. A few days later I called again; Mom was busy talking and planning the next move and Dad was silent. Mom had already told my sister and brothers. Everyone was in shock but ready to help me.

Mom said to me, "In a year this will all be behind you, and you can live a normal life."

That sounded good to me – living a normal life – but there were a lot of hurdles to cross before "normal" happened.

I called home every few days, and soon my sister Janet and her husband John and my brother Fred decided to take action. If I sent them a resume`, they would fix it up and send it out to prospective employers with the hope that I would have some interviews lined up when I got home. I was grateful and relieved again. For the first time since Mary broke the news almost a month ago, I had a plan. I got busy right away putting together a resume`. I began to feel a glimmer of hope. Fred and John reworked the document into something that looked halfway decent and started sending it out in Toledo, Dayton, and Cincinnati. I never asked, and I didn't care where they sent it. I was willing to sweep floors if I had to.

Meanwhile, Customs released the car. I picked it up and headed back to Binga with an overnight in Bulawayo to talk to Mary. She had spoken to her parents; whose reaction was predictably similar. She told me her mother had called me a "rotter."

When I looked a little confused, she said, "It's Australian slang for a despicable person."

Ouch! She thought that in time they would come to accept us, but I was glad we decided to move to America since I wasn't sure what Australians did to rotters. Mary was getting ready to go to Leeds in a few weeks. I left for Binga feeling relieved and worried about what was going to happen next.

When I got back to the mission, Mike and I decided it was time to call Bishop Hoffman. One evening, with Mike sitting right next to me, I made the call and read to him the same little speech I'd read to my parents a week earlier. There was shocked silence.

"Your decision seems pretty hasty Mike," he said. "Don't you think you should take more time to think about this."

"I've thought about this for a long time, Jim," I said, "this is something I want to do and have been wanting to do since I was in college."

"I don't know what to say, Mike," he said, "I am staring out the window. I am stunned. Put the other Mike on the phone please."

Mike took the phone and then after a minute said, "Jim wants to talk to me alone now. Go into my bedroom and close the door."

From Mike's back bedroom I could hear muffled sounds of their talking. When they hung up, Mike told me that the Bishop reamed him out for letting me go off on my own to Perth with Mary. After he had finished ranting, Mike asked him, "And how was I supposed to stop a guy who is a foot taller than I am, weighs 50 pounds more than I do, and is deeply in love?"

The Bishop, knowing there was nothing anyone could have done, told him he needed someone to yell at and Mike was convenient. After that, I wrote a letter and sent it out to my friends to tell them the news. I sent out over 100 letters. The one person we decided not to tell Bishop Prieto. I'd leave that to Bishop Hoffman after I was gone.

Chapter 28

Waiting to Go April 1989

———————

At the beginning of April, I took the big green bus again to Bulawayo to meet Mary. I stayed in my hotel since I wasn't able to show my face at the convent anymore. Mary had announced to all the sisters that she was leaving the convent and going to England for a while to work as a physical therapist until she could figure out what to do next, but only Sr. Eileen and one other sister knew the whole story. I planned to go with Mary to Harare so we could spend a few days together before she flew to England. Late the next morning I went to the bus stop and waited. In a few minutes, I saw the VW Golf pull into the parking lot with Mary and Eileen. It was the same car Mary, and I had used for our trips out to Matopos and for our dinner dates.

"Hello Eileen," I said, "I guess this is it."

"Yes. I hope you are ready for what comes next," Eileen said.

I waited a moment, and Eileen gave Mary a big hug and then she turned and looked at me.

"Come here," she told me. I walked over, and she gave me a long hug and whispered in my ear, "You'll be fine."

Mary gave her bags to the driver, and as we were about to board the bus, Eileen said, "I feel like the mother giving away the bride."

We were so embarrassed about the whole situation that neither of us found her comment that funny. She waved at us as the bus pulled out of the parking lot. She seemed happy for us.

We talked the whole way to Harare. It felt good to be making plans for our life together. I told her about my resume`s and that I hoped Fred and John could get an employer to bite. We walked from the coach to the Russell Hotel; an apartment building converted into a hotel. It gave us a kitchen and stove, so we didn't have to eat out for every meal. It was also big enough to store the shopping Mary planned to do. We spent the next four days in Harare buying clothes. Up until now, Mary wore brown and beige skirts and blouses, the modified habit all the sisters wore that distinguished them as Franciscans. Brown was their color since St. Julitta wore brown. Back home in the parish, I wore black pants and a black clerical shirt with a white collar. In Zimbabwe, I wore khaki all the time. We both looked forward to adding a little more color to our wardrobes. We spent the next three days going to every thrift store we could find shopping for skirts, blouses, and jewelry so that Mary had something to wear when she arrived in Leeds to begin life outside the convent. I enjoyed helping her pick out clothes. We shopped during the day, rested in the afternoon, found a little restaurant in the evening and talked and talked about our new life together. Even with all the difficult things ahead, that sounded great - our new life together.

Mike was also in Harare at that time; he was heading back to Toledo to take his three months of leave. He and I planned to meet up there for a final time where he'd give me the keys to the Land Cruiser to drive back to Binga. The afternoon before he left we met at a local hotel, and we drank a final beer together as teammates.

"Well buddy," he said to me, "this is it. I'm not sure what to say except I'm going to miss you a lot. I hope you and Mary are really happy together."

We talked about all we accomplished in the three and a half years he had been there and laughed about the nights it was so hot and quiet that we could sit out on the front porch in Binga wearing only our underwear and drinking a beer.

"Good luck buddy," were his final words to me.

We hugged, and I drove the Land Cruiser back to the hotel where Mary and I were staying. I was saying goodbye to a way of life and to the people who knew me as a priest. I was trading in that identity for a new identity as a husband and father, which felt genuine. I felt lighter as I shed the heavy weight of pretending to be happy and thought, I didn't know I was allowed to be this happy. The next day I drove Mary to the airport for her trip to England.

As we waited for her plane to board, Mary looked at me and said, "I'll be able to work a lot of temporary physical therapist assignments while I'm in England and at least pay my rent to Eileen's brother and family. Maybe I'll be able to save some money for when we get together in America." Neither of us knew how long it would take for me to get a job once I got back home in another ten weeks. I drove out of the airport and headed for Bulawayo where I stopped for the night. It was lonely being there knowing that Mary was gone. I ate dinner in the hotel dining room, and the next morning I left for Binga. I told Mike I would cover the mission for him until another priest could be found to replace me. But I could only stay until the middle of May. Then I had to get home and get on with finding a job and a place to live. Now with Mike in Toledo and Mary in Leeds, the next ten weeks in Binga would be tough. I wished I could have gone sooner to get things ready for Mary and the baby, but I'd disappointed enough people already, so I decided to stay and keep things going at the mission. I prayed the Universe would look kindly on my willingness to stick it out instead of rushing home.

Once back in Binga, I continued to go to the outstations and visit, but my mind and heart were no longer in the ministry. I was worried about everything I had to do before the baby arrived in August. Out in Nakangala, I stayed in our brand new house. What a difference from the ramshackle hut I stayed at in Kalungwizi when I first arrived over five years earlier. The new house was beautiful with its white plastered walls inside and the white stucco on the outside. The thick thatching gave the interior a fresh and cozy feel, and the little windows let in enough light to see during the day. I set up my cot and mosquito netting and sat in the camp chair feeling safe and comfortable. I walked the roads alone for hours, wondering what this new life was going to be like and what work I would do. The moon was so bright one evening that even in the darkness I could see the road and the rondavels in each small village I passed. It struck me that this was what I learned on that retreat - Look to the Light! I missed so many opportunities in the past to live a different life because I was so caught up in my darkness - a suffering victim, helpless, hostage, and "doing time." Now "looking to the light" I finally said "Yes" to this new chance at happiness. But what was I getting myself into now? No job. No home. No experience. Six years earlier I came to Zimbabwe, a stranger with no home and no experience, to a land, culture, and language I didn't know. Now I was about to do the same thing. As long as I kept "looking to the light," I felt an inner confidence and trust in myself and in the same higher forces that had helped me before. I remembered the many nights talking to Mike, the mornings writing in my journal, the days opening up to Mary as we spent time together, and the ten days of retreat - finally facing my inner demons I felt free to make a new choice. Walking in the bright light on this dirt road in Nakangala all of my senses felt alive. I saw clearly the rocky bluffs in the distance and the smoke rising from the cooking fires in every village. I could smell the animals and the woody scent from the fires. I listened to the sound of drumming and singing. I felt peaceful with this inner light to guide me even with so much unknown.

I felt sorry for Jules who was stuck with me alone in Binga. Every evening we sat on the front porch of my house and drank beer, but I was not much for conversation during that time. It was hard to picture what married life would be like; having a job, and living in an apartment with a new baby. I had entered the seminary in high school and lived like a priest ever since. It was the only way of life I knew. But in the midst of the shock, confusion, worry, and fear the slightest glimmer of excitement broke through. One word kept coming to me -- Relief! More than anything, I felt relieved that this long time of feigning happiness was drawing to a close. I kept saying, "I didn't know I was allowed to be this happy." I began to feel energized, renewed, and freed from my self-imposed prison by an event that was an accident but led to a life I had always wanted. I was going to have my family.

That image of myself in the coffin kept coming back to me - here lies a wasted life. And I understood that what I was doing was not the wasted life, but that I experienced no joy in what I did. I was making choices focused on my joy and happiness. A new way of living was opening up for me as I let go of the dark thoughts, the poor me, and "looked to the light."

As I embraced the shocking news of Mary's pregnancy, the shameful feelings of having disappointed friends, family, and the Bishop, and the fear of how I was going to provide for Mary and the baby, I realized that this was the passage I had to go through to get to my new life. Just as I had needed help when I first arrived in Zimbabwe; orienting to the mission life that came in so many unexpected ways, I hoped for the same assistance to navigate this passage because it looked just as scary.

After I'd been home a while, I went to confession and told the priest, "Father, I am sorry for how much hurt I caused to others and for what I did. But I am not sorry for the way it turned out. I feel happy." To which the old priest replied, "God writes straight with crooked lines." I felt the way the woman who had been caught in adultery must have felt in the Gospel story when after all those left who were going to stone her, Jesus said to her, "Neither do I condemn you. Go in peace."

Chapter 29

The Lakes

Finally, the day arrived for me to leave – May 19, 1989 - just a little over three months since Mary discovered she was pregnant. Jules and I went to Kamitivi for a farewell dinner with Julitta. Both of these women were so gentle and generous. Julitta and I reminisced about the early days of the mission.

"Remember the first time we got together as a team, just after you were chosen. Marge cooked a big breakfast for us all, and you came a half hour late. She was so angry at you," Julitta said.

We spent the evening remembering adventures. We avoided talking about the fact that I was leaving the mission, leaving them, and going into an unknown future. We had all grown close over the course of the past three and a half years and Julitta, and I had worked together since the beginning. The next day, they took me to the Dette airport for the flight to Harare.

Jules said, "I'm going to miss you."

I hugged each of them and then walked through the gate. There were no dry eyes on this farewell. As the plane lifted off, I could see them through the window, and we waved. Then they turned to go back to Binga, and the plane banked to take me to a new life.

The flight to Harare took a little over 90 minutes. As I looked down over the bush, I remembered my last night in Nakangala. The people put on an impromptu going-away party for me. The people of Binga had a going away party for me on May 16. I hadn't planned any goodbye parties because I couldn't stop worrying about everything I needed to accomplish before the baby arrived, and I felt grateful for their expressions of love and admiration. I would have been happy to slip out of the country. How strange that Marge and I who were the first two people here, the ones who started the whole mission, would leave in such a hidden way. But those were the circumstances. No one knew the real reason for my leaving. The Tongas were used to Europeans coming and going. Most of the Europeans I came to know at the beginning were back home now or on to new assignments. The Tongas accepted this as the way of life. The celebration at Nakangala was not an all-nighter as the one at Kalungwizi had been when I first went there almost five years earlier. Lemonth Muleya, who was the first one to take me around the villages back in 1984 when I stayed in Kalungwizi, gave a heartfelt farewell and at the end said something that touched me.

He said, "I hope that one day I can preach as well as Bafada Syamuunda."

I never knew how well I communicated in Tonga. Lemonth, with these simple words, spoke to my heart and gave me a great gift. These people had adopted me, and we had helped one another find a new path and greater independence.

I spent my last night in Africa in Harare. And as I walked around the city I remembered the early trips there with Marge to get our papers and organize our car. The many times I spent with the German Dominican Sisters and how kind and hospitable they had been. I remembered meeting Mom and Dad and Fred at the airport and Dad holding up the yellow bag from the duty-free shop and the bottles of bourbon we shared. Bishop Hoffman had come through that airport to see me many times.

And welcoming Mike and Jules there had helped me through one of the roughest periods of my life. The city held so many memories, not the least of which were the times Mary and I spent there together. Now I felt released from my self-imposed life sentence, freed to step into the light of a new life. I regretted the friendships I would lose as a result of my decision, but I could not regret making a decision for my happiness.

The next day I boarded my overnight flight for London. After a brief layover where I took the time to wash up and change clothes, I boarded the short flight for Leeds. After months of waiting and worry, Mary was there waiting for me in the terminal just like Perth. And even though I had never been to Leeds, it felt like I was coming home again because I was coming to be with Mary. She looked beautiful.

Mary ran up to me, threw her arms around me and said, "I love you, darling."

I felt the worry and anxiety of the past months melt away. I loved Mary more than ever with her tiny pregnant stomach. "You are glowing," I said. And we hugged and kissed again. The journey was almost over; just a few small steps remained – getting a job, getting a place to live, getting furniture, getting a car, getting married, and getting ready to have a baby. OK, maybe not so small, but we were together now, and it felt possible. Bring it on, I thought!

Three months passed since I had last seen Mary in Harare. I didn't know how long it would take me to send for her once I returned to Ohio, so we decided to spend a week together in the Lake District in England. Mary rented a Ford Fiesta and booked a little apartment for our holiday using the money she made working as a physical therapist for the past few months. The drive from the airport to the Lake District was beautiful, and everything was shimmering again for me. We were soon out in the countryside. It all looked familiar because of the time I spent in Liverpool in 1976, but this area of England was breathtaking.

We drove through picturesque villages, landscapes with lakes and boats, and tree-covered hills that could have come right out of a painting. The farmyards there were neat as a pin, with stone fences encircling every field.

Our little apartment was built on the back of a beautiful, old, two-story whitewashed home along a winding road deep in the countryside. It had a gorgeous view of the surrounding hills and fields. It felt like we were in another world. We walked through the entrance to the apartment at the back of the house and into a little kitchen with a little table and two chairs. Then we walked into a little sitting room with a loveseat, coffee table, chair, and TV. At the end of the love seat, we climbed a tiny ladder that led to a little loft filled with a king size bed. A skylight in the ceiling provided light. It felt perfect.

After we had unpacked, I sat outside overlooking the view and smoking a cigar, relieved that we had made it this far. I couldn't have felt happier, more peaceful, more serene, or more alive. Even though I had nothing, I felt like I had gained everything and I experienced a profound certainty it would all work out. I wanted to savor this moment of freedom; I didn't want to miss a second of anything. I had postponed living for so long. Now I had received a second chance at happiness, and I felt grateful.

That evening we went to a pub for dinner, and I drank a pint of beer and smoked another cigar. The oak-beamed ceiling, along with the dark mahogany wood of the bar and tables and the burgundy upholstering of the chairs, made it feel like we were walking into a Dickens novel. Paintings of the area lined the walls. Mary and I loved being there together, and I couldn't take my eyes off of her. I leaned over and gave her a kiss. Each day we stopped into a different pub because each one was so unique. We had fun deciding which pub to visit each evening. Everything was fun with Mary.

We enjoyed looking for a different walking trail that took us through various parts of the area. The Lake District is notorious for being socked in with rain and fog for weeks on end. During the few days we stayed there, it only rained a couple of times and never when we were walking. By now Mary was six months pregnant, so we had to take it slow and rest whenever we found a bench along one of the trails. But she insisted we take walks every day we could because she wanted me to experience the beauty of the area. The Lake District is only 35 square miles, yet packed into that area are lakes and mountains, some reaching 3000 feet. At every bend in the road, we found another breathtaking view. Roundabouts sprang up at every crossroads which I found challenging to navigate. Rather than stop signs or traffic lights, these roundabouts provided a steady flow of traffic for drivers who knew how to manage them. The trick to negotiating a roundabout involved timing and turn-signaling correctly. Mary warned me about them as I approached the first roundabout of my life.

She sounded like an air traffic controller, "Now slow down on your approach into the roundabout. Check to your right to see if there is any traffic coming. You look clear to the right so proceed into the roundabout. Now signal to the left your intention to move through, now signal right."

It would not be unusual for me to make a few trips around the circle before finally figuring out which road she wanted me to take. Mary varied between being infuriated at my lack of concentration, and giggling helplessly beside me as I made yet another trip around the circle yelling, "Abort!"

On one beautiful day, we decided to take a boat ride to the end of one of the lakes and then walk back to town. As the boat went further and further down the lake, I marveled at the beautiful scenery and worried about how far we had to walk to get back to the car. When we disembarked, a path lead straight up a steep hill, then another steep hill and another. We stopped and rested at almost every bench we found along the way, but by the time we reached the end of the walk, we felt exhausted, and Mary was famished. I ran to the car, got the picnic we brought with us and ran back to Mary. She was so hungry that before I could unpack the food, she reached in, grabbed a roll and jammed it into her mouth. We decided to skip the pub that day.

Each day we went into the town of Keswick to shop for our supper and wander around. There were a few jewelers there, and we decided to buy our wedding rings since we didn't know when we would have the opportunity again. Not only would the rings symbolize our love and commitment, but also serve as a reminder of another beautiful moment in our lives. Each small decision we made took me closer and closer to living the life I had always dreamed of living. We choose two simple gold bands. They had to be sized and then sent to Mary who would bring them with her to Toledo.

On the only rainy day, we drove to Leeds where Mary had a prenatal appointment with her doctor. The rain didn't bother us. Nothing bothered us much because we were doing everything together now.

On Sunday we went to Mass at Our Lady of the Lakes. It was an old brownstone building right in the middle of town. In the afternoon we took another walk, this time reading poetry from William Wordsworth who lived in the Lake District and was inspired by its beauty. We bought a leather bound edition of his poetry in a bookshop in town and then carried it with us. Whenever we found a bench with a beautiful view, we'd sit and read a poem.

We walked by Windermere, Coniston, Grasmere, Ullswater, each place more beautiful than the last. It felt like Camelot. Time stopped for us there again, like it stopped for us in Perth. For that week, we felt protected and safe. But soon it was time to get back to reality and the tasks facing me at home. We spent two days with the family who provided housing and support for Mary. On the last night Sr. Eileen's brother and his wife took us out to a nice restaurant for dinner.

Eileen's brother, Pat, offered a little advice, "Mike, get a house as soon as you can. You'll never regret it."

I just hoped I could get a job and an apartment. The next day I said goodbye to Mary for the last time in my life and flew to London where I caught a connecting flight to Detroit. It had been almost four months since Mary delivered the news, "I'm pregnant," sitting in my little room at the convent in Bulawayo. Now I was sitting on a plane headed for home where I could finally get busy getting things ready for Mary and the baby. As the plane landed in Detroit, I knew this was going to be a different kind of homecoming than I ever experienced before.

Chapter 30

Facing the Music

N o crowd of family and friends waited to greet me in Detroit when I landed on Monday, May 29. John and Janet stood alone at the arrival gate. I felt a bit sheepish as I hugged and kissed them. No longer the big brother who accomplished so much, I was the prodigal brother who fell from grace and now needed his baby sister to help him figure out the basics of living.

On the drive back to Toledo, we talked about job possibilities, where I would live, and how Mom and Dad were doing. John and Janet had lined up two interviews for me. John told me that there were a lot of jobs available and not to worry. We stopped into their neighborhood bar for something to eat and a few beers to fortify me for my meeting with Mom and Dad. They were both still trying to deal with my sudden decision to leave the priesthood and Mary's pregnancy.

John looked at me and said, "What was it like on your ordination day?"

"It was the worst day of my life," I said.

John ordered another round of beer for us all. After an hour, I couldn't put it off any longer, and they drove me home.

The front door was open, so I carried my bags up the front sidewalk and through the screen door right into the living room. Dad got up first from his big chair and gave me a hug. Then Mom hugged me too.

"We're so glad to see you, Mickey," she said.

Dad just looked on, neither of us knowing what to say. I took my bags up to my old bedroom, then came back downstairs to the living room.

"What are you going to do now?" Mom asked.

"It looks like John and Fred have a couple of interviews lined up so first thing in the morning I'm going to set up times with them."

Mom was a worrier even in good times. I could see how anxious and upset she felt. "John told me there are lots of jobs now. I just have to find one."

"How's Mary doing?" Mom said.

"She's occasionally working as a physical therapist now that the baby is bigger. She's living with a lovely family in Leeds waiting for me to call her to come to America." Dad sat quietly.

"You've got a lot to do." Mom said.

I nodded and then went up to my old bedroom to unpack. We'd lived in this house since I was a baby and this bedroom held memories of growing up and of homecomings from College, Rome, and Africa. Now I hoped it would become a launching pad for me into the next chapter of my life.

The next morning, Tuesday, I woke early and began calling the prospective employers John and Fred had found. I focused all of my energy and attention on one thing: Get a job and send for Mary. This task consumed me. I also arranged to meet Bishop Hoffman for a final time and to see my best friends Bernie and Nancy.

I scheduled an interview on Wednesday evening for a position as house manager at the Ronald McDonald House in Toledo. The job involved managing the home and being available for families who stayed there while their children were being treated for cancer. I wasn't particularly handy with repairs, but counseling and consoling families are what I did as a priest. The job also came with a small apartment since the house manager was expected to live on site, a part of the job that did not appeal to me. The house sat right in the middle of Toledo, and I wasn't sure how comfortable I felt being that close to the Cathedral and accessible to everyone who'd known me as a priest.

I arrived for the interview at 6:30 in the evening and met with a large group of men and women, members of the board of directors responsible for hiring the new house manager. I had never interviewed for a job before, so I felt a little intimidated and worried that people might recognize me. They explained the job and the responsibilities, and I asked questions. I told them a bit about my background, and as they began to look at my resume` and ask about my education, I pointed out to them that I had been a priest, something none of them had realized. They still had a few more candidates to interview and promised to call me.

My second interview was on Thursday afternoon near Delphos, Ohio at a foster care agency for a case manager position to visit children in their foster homes. I liked the idea of it being far enough away to have some space, yet close enough to my family in Toledo. At the first interview, I discovered that the job came with a car, a Yugo and that it involved working from home. I had never heard of that brand of car before. One of the supervisors took me out to the parking lot and showed me a car that looked like a cross between a golf cart and a Ford Fiesta.

"It's made in Yugoslavia," he said.

I felt glad I wouldn't have to worry about a car if I got the job. Working from home and having a car provided were both big pluses in my book. Also, the hours were flexible although often involved work in the evenings to see the children. That wasn't bad either.

On Friday morning, I received a call to schedule a second round of interviews in Delphos for the following Tuesday. I felt excited about the potential of landing a job so soon. I heard nothing from the Ronald

MacDonald House people. I didn't have any other interviews lined up, although I scoured the papers every day.

On Friday I also arranged to meet with Hoffman for our farewell conversation. He told me that we could spend the evening at his lakeside cottage, a 30-minute drive from Toledo in Michigan.

"Mike, pick me up at my office, and we'll drive up there together," he said.

I had served as the Associate Pastor and the Administrator at the Cathedral before I went to Africa. I knew everyone who worked in the building and most people in the neighborhood, so I felt a little sheepish as I drove down Parkwood Ave and pulled into the drive outside the building. The bishop stood out near the street, dressed in "civvies," waiting for me.

As I pulled up, he jumped into the car and said, "Let's get out of here."

It all seemed very undercover, but I suppose he wanted to make the situation more comfortable for me. Like my homecoming earlier in the week, I felt a little awkward as we drove away, but by the time we reached I 75 and were heading north, he was chatting away about my plans and asking about my last few months in Zimbabwe. It felt a little like that drive we'd taken together almost six years earlier when he'd asked me about going to Africa. Now he was asking me about the next chapter in my life; concerned, interested, and offering me his love and support.

We spent time at the cottage looking at the lake and drinking beer and talking about the old times at Cathedral, my experiences in Africa, and what I planned to do next. I said, "Jim, I feel sorry that I've let you down and everyone else."

He looked at me and said, "Shane, you've been busy helping people all your life. Focus on yourself and your family now. Do something different. Be a bartender or something."

I laughed and told him I applied for foster care job. We grilled steaks, looked out at the lake, and enjoyed our last few moments as colleagues.

After dinner, I dropped him back at the Cathedral, and we said our "good-byes." The next week, the Bishop announced in the Catholic newspaper, the Catholic Chronicle, that I had been granted a leave of absence "for personal reasons." My leave of absence would be the first step in a process that took three years to complete and involved a dispensation from my vow of celibacy that only the Pope could issue. (Pope John Paul II did grant it in February 1992 when I was officially dispensed from all of my vows.) Until then, in the eyes of the church, I was a black sheep.

On Tuesday (8 days since I'd arrived home) I drove back to Delphos for the second interview. The receptionist showed me into a large conference room where five supervisors had already gathered. After the introduction, they told me to sit on one side of a large conference table. They asked me about my background and why I thought I could work as a foster care case manager. They asked me about my experience with children who were abused, neglected, or dependent. What I would do if there were a problem at one of the foster homes and the parents did not want the child anymore. I tried my best to answer them, but this was harder than the first meeting, and I didn't know how to answer many of the questions they posed. Afterward, I met with the director again, and he asked me if there were any of my references that I preferred he didn't call. I told him he could call them all. My reference list included the Bishop of the Diocese of Toledo and Rev. Bernard Boff. I hoped they would give me a good recommendation. He promised to get back to me in a few days about the job. As I drove back to Toledo, I wasn't sure how the interview had gone, so in the meantime, I decided to keep looking.

On Friday, June 9, (11 days after I arrived home), I got a call offering me the job in Delphos for an annual salary of $18,500, the highest they could provide me with that position, and the use of a car – the Yugo. Mom and I sat at the kitchen table working out a budget to decide whether I could support my new small family on that amount. We decided I could do it, but it would be tight, so I called them back and accepted. The position was available immediately, but I said that I was available after July 4 since

I needed time to get the rest of my life in order and to get Mary here. They told me to come to Delphos at some point to sign the papers and then come for orientation. I had accomplished the first big hurdle. I had a job. Now I needed a place to live.

Janet became my surrogate mother and offered to help me find an apartment. First thing Monday morning (14 days after my arrival home) we began looking at apartments in Bluffton since I wanted to live near Delphos. There was little available there, so we moved our search to Lima. We had no idea where to begin to look and drove around hoping to see a "for rent" sign. We found a couple of places that looked nice, but the nice places were all full. Finally, one rental manager recommended a more country-type setting near Elida. We drove out of Lima and into farmland that was nearer to Delphos. We pulled into a small subdivision full of ranch-style apartments. The manager showed us an apartment with two large bedrooms, a living room and kitchen that connected and a back door that opened out onto a yard and a farmer's field beyond. We loved it. After a little negotiating and assurance that I had a job, I made a down payment and signed the lease. The apartment was 20 minutes from my new office. Janet and I celebrated with a drink at a hotel in Findlay on the way back to Toledo. I felt relieved that the three biggest hurdles were out of the way; a job, an apartment, and a car - well, a Yugo!

The next day, Tuesday, June 13 (15 days after I arrived home) I called Mary and told her I had a job and a place to live, and she should arrange to fly over as soon as she could. Things were moving faster than I ever imagined. I couldn't wait to be reunited with Mary at last.

On Wednesday, Mom and Dad and I went out to garage sales to look for furniture. By now dad was used to the whirlwind I was creating with my job search, my apartment find, and now looking for furniture. At one garage sale, mom bought a glass-topped table with four chairs for our dining room.

"Here's my wedding present for you two," she said.

At the second, I met a guy whose fiancé had ordered him to get rid of all his stuff. I bought him out of a whole condo's worth of kitchen supplies and dishes as well as his entire bedroom suite. Janet gave me a couch. I already had a rocking chair. We brought everything home and stored it in the garage until I could move it into our new place on the following Saturday. Mary called on Thursday (17 days from arrival) and told me she booked a flight and would arrive a week from Wednesday in Detroit.

My good friend Dan and his wife Dee connected me with the Lutheran Pastor who had performed their marriage a few years earlier. He was the hospital chaplain at St. Luke's Hospital. I met with Fr. Paul, and he agreed to do the wedding after I explained my unusual circumstances. I gave him a few readings I thought were appropriate and we set a date for Thursday, June 22, the day after Mary arrived in America. I also reserved a restaurant in Waterville for our post-wedding dinner reception.

I rented a big Ryder truck, and my brother Don and I drove all over Toledo picking up my stuff from the Cathedral Rectory, a mattress and frame from Banner Mattress, and the things I had been given or bought at garage sales. On Saturday (19 days after arrival) dad and I got in the truck, and the whole family drove to Elida to help me move in. Tina, Fred's wife, brought a curtain box with her and besides moving the furniture, setting up the kitchen, installing the TV that Dad gave us as his wedding present, we also hung curtains. It looked beautiful and homey.

We got back to Mom and Dad's, and I could finally rest and wait for Mary to arrive in a few days. In just under three weeks I had accomplished everything I had worried about for the previous three months. It was a miracle no one could believe. Even Dad started to get excited.

Chapter 31

Mary Arrives

———

On Wednesday evening, June 21, 1989 (24 days after I left her at the airport in Leeds) Mary landed at the Detroit Airport, the last step into our new life together. It took Mary quite a while to get through customs and into the terminal lobby, and when she finally walked out, she looked exhausted. Once we were in the car and on our way, I could tell her about everything I had accomplished in the last three weeks. After jumping through all of the hurdles over the past four months, we could relax knowing that we would be together for good. I had met her and left her so many times in the previous three years that I could hardly believe she wasn't here just for a visit.

We ate supper at Bob Evans. While we waited for the waitress to bring our dinner, I casually said, "Our wedding is scheduled for 6:00 tomorrow evening."

"What?"

"Well, I wanted to make sure you didn't have time to change your mind," I said.

She looked at me across the table with that sly smile and said, "Luckily, I bought a dress in Leeds for the wedding, but I didn't think I'd need it the day after I arrived! I'm glad we're doing this right away. I've waited too long for this day." Her surprise turned into excitement.

I kept thinking - How do you spell 'relief'? And that is what I felt, both a profound relief that my self-imposed sentence of "doing time" was coming to an end and that the life I always wanted to live was about to begin. I felt grateful for this second chance at happiness.

Thursday morning, we got up, ate breakfast at the nearby Friendly's and then took off to the courthouse to get the marriage license. As we drove into Toledo, I pointed out the sights of the city. We passed by the zoo and were soon in the middle of downtown Toledo. We parked in front of the courthouse and walked up the steps and into the main lobby. The courthouse was huge, and we eventually found a sign for "marriage licenses" pointing to the second floor. There were a lot of people there that day, and we waited in line for half an hour. When it was our turn to fill out the paperwork, the clerk refused to accept the address on my driver's license.

She said, "I know this address. It's the address of a church and not a residence. You'll have to produce a residential address in Lucas County."

I tried to explain that it was a residential address without mentioning that it was a rectory and that I had been a priest living there at the time. She still refused to give us the license. I couldn't believe it. After all we'd been through, this clerk was standing in the way of my whole future life. Back down to the lobby, out the door, down the steps, we almost ran to the car. "We've got to get home, look for something with an address on it and get back here." I wasn't sure if I could find the document the clerk needed or even if she would accept what I would produce.

We raced back to Mom and Dad's house to look for a bill, or an envelope addressed to me in Lucas County. I ran in the back door with Mary in tow and shouted out as I passed by, "Mom and Sad, this is Mary. I have to find an envelope with my address on it right now." I disappeared up the stairs into my old room to find something with my name and my home address to prove that I lived in Lucas County in the past six months, leaving Mary to introduce herself to my parents. I rooted around in old credit card bills, hoping to find one that hadn't been shredded already. My heart pounded as I picked up envelope after envelope. What if I couldn't find anything? Then I saw it. An envelope from Visa that Mom saved for me with my name and my Lucas County address and the date stamp of May 12, 1989. I ran down the stairs holding the envelope in one hand, grabbed Mary with the other and yelled over my shoulder, "Gotta go. See you in an hour." And we took off for the courthouse. This time the clerk accepted my proof of residency and issued us the marriage license.

We drove back home again for a more relaxed introduction and a lovely luncheon that Mom had produced as a welcome for her future daughter-in-law. We spent the afternoon chatting and laughing about their first introduction, and everything we'd been through in the past four months. By this time, Dad had come to accept the situation, found himself enchanted by Mary, and was his old jolly self.

At 5:00 we arrived at the chapel at St. Luke's Hospital in Maumee. We found our way to the chapel that was a small room with an altar and a picture of Jesus hanging on the back wall. There were a few wooden chairs with cloth seats. Fr. Paul came out and took Mary and I back to his office for a few minutes. That constituted our pre-marriage counseling. Dan Williams was my best man and my sister, Janet, the matron of honor. Mom and Dad and Don and Joan, Dan's wife Dee and Janet's husband John made up the entire guest list for the wedding. It was small, intimate and just perfect. To our surprise, Fr. Paul changed the reading from the one I picked and replaced it with one from the Gospel of John where Jesus repeats over and over to his disciples, "Remain in my love." When Mary and I first met, I talked about this very passage at Mass with the sisters one day, and after Mass, Mary and I talked about it more. Some couples have their special song. This passage was special to us, and now here it was showing up at our wedding. We took it as a blessing. After a few pictures and thanks to Fr. Paul for his help, we headed off for dinner.

The restaurant was full of antique furniture decorated in the style of an Inn from the late 1800's. We all sat at a large table and enjoyed an excellent meal. Mary and I were married and starting our life together. Afterward, we spent our wedding night at a Holiday Inn but were too exhausted from the adventures of the past few months to do anything but go to bed. The next day we drove to Elida. I couldn't wait to show Mary our apartment.

Chapter 32

Life in Lima

———————

The next morning, Friday, we drove to Elida. Mary told me she felt a bit nervous about the apartment I managed to find in such a short time. She'd imagined some dark and dirty hovel in the midst of the inner city. I picked a route that took us through the country, then through the village of Elida and out to our subdivision.

When we turned onto the road, she said, "This is nice."

I pulled up to our building and parked in our parking spot behind our apartment. "This is our new home, darling," I said. "I would carry you over the threshold, but you've gotten a little large."

She cuffed me on the back of the head and said, "Open the door, wise guy." Then she said, "This is beautiful. How did you do it?"

She was flabbergasted as she walked around our furnished, two-bedroom country apartment. She couldn't believe how nice and light and clean it was. She walked around and kept saying over and over, "This is beautiful." I could see the tension and worry and anxiety of the past four months drain out of her. Carrying the baby for all this time and not knowing when or where she would finally land was exhausting. She asked me if it was OK to drink the water.

"This is America, not Africa. Of course, it is OK to drink the water," I scoffed. A few moments later, someone slipped a notice under the door that said there had been a problem with the water and we should boil it first before drinking. I knew right then I was getting the sideways stare but didn't dare to look up. Right after that, there was a knock at the door. When I answered it, there was a nun I had worked with in Toledo who popped over to welcome us. She lived a few doors down. Maybe we weren't going to be so anonymous. Over the course of the next few months, we had some visitors, including one of the African priests from Hwange Diocese who was visiting Toledo. I think people wanted to see if we were OK, and everyone left with a sense that everything was just fine. One friend told me, "I believe you have actually found your vocation." I never felt happier, and as time progressed that happiness and feeling of "rightness" only deepened.

We spent ten days together shopping, marketing, and getting used to married life before I began my job. During that time, we set up an appointment with a doctor so Mary could continue her prenatal visits. The baby was due in two months.

The OB-GYN in Lima expressed his concern about Mary's age. She was 36 years old with her first baby and already well into her third trimester. But an ultrasound showed the baby looked fine. At the beginning of August, just weeks before the due date, we took a prenatal class at St. Rita's along with a lot of other first time parents. Most of them were in their early 20's, and we were conspicuously older, in our late 30's. Oh well, we thought, better late than never! Now with everything else put into place, we focused on the birth.

I went to my new job orientation and received five foster families from all over northwest Ohio. The previous caseworker handed me her files in a brown paper sack. It took me a few weeks to figure out what she had done in the past months. It didn't matter. I was happy to have a job, a place to live, and a doctor to help with the birth. That was what mattered to me. Driving to my weekly visits in my little Yugo gave me a chance just to relax and get reacquainted with Ohio.

It turned out to be the perfect job for me. I could work from home and spend a lot of time with Mary. I worked hard the first part of the week, visiting my families and making case notes, and then had a more relaxed end of the week and a long weekend. We took advantage of the time we had, walking and exploring parks, and playing games together. We were enjoying a quiet life and restoring ourselves from the trauma and challenges of the past six months.

As the weeks progressed, the baby grew, and Mary became more and more uncomfortable. Soon the baby was overdue. We had just gone to bed at 9:30 PM on August 31when Mary announced that her water had broken and that it was time to go to the hospital. In the previous weeks, we practiced different routes to the hospital. Mary packed a hospital bag so she'd be ready to go at a moment's notice. She grabbed it now, jumped into the Yugo, and we drove to St. Rita's.

Mary still wasn't quite dilated enough and even though she was having contractions labor progressed very slowly. So we walked the halls to get things rolling. Hours passed while the baby took its own sweet time. Mary lay in bed in the pain of contractions and the worry about giving birth. As I sat beside her, my mind and my attention wandered off to the TV just above the bed, where Jay Leno was doing his monolog. I was quickly drawn back to reality when I heard a sharp,

"Turn that damn TV off," followed by a very stern lecture about my lack of sensitivity. "How could you watch TV when I am laying here in pain?"

Here were my beautiful bride and the soon-to-be mother of our child, cussing at me in this sacred moment. Little did I know just how long and painful this whole process would be.

Ten hours passed and the baby wasn't moving. That morning, Dr. Ryan began preparing for a C-Section since he was worried that Mary had been in labor for too long, but just as we were making preparations for the operation, the labor contractions returned in earnest, and the doctor quickly moved Mary into the delivery room. At that point, everything became a bit of a blur.

Mary pushed and pushed but the baby just wasn't moving correctly, and now the doctor worried about both her and the child. So Dr. Ryan used some pretty serious hardware to yank the baby out. Before long there was a cry and we saw our little girl. At 1:00 PM on September 1, 1989, Mary and I became parents.

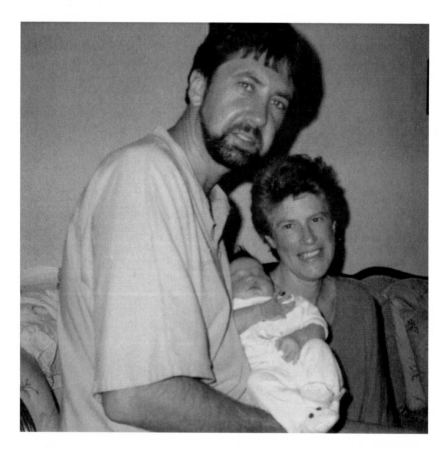

After a while, the nurses and doctor left us alone with the baby. Mary was utterly exhausted from the whole ordeal, from her discovery she was pregnant on February 10 in Bulawayo Zimbabwe, and then onto Leeds England where she worked and lived with strangers who became like surrogate parents, to Toledo and getting married, and now to Elida Ohio USA. It had been an unbelievable ride, but we made it. And here was a baby girl. Exhausted, Mary asked me what we should name her.

I went through the list of names that we'd picked out together and finally said, "She looks like a Stephanie to me." And so she was.

We had two days in the hospital. When it was time to leave, I pulled our little Yugo up to the front doors where the nurse was standing with Mary and Stephanie. She helped us put Stephanie into the car seat and wished us well. This was the scariest part of the whole process for me. We were on our own now with a new baby. But I knew that together Mary and I could conquer anything. As I drove very slowly out of St. Rita's and toward our new home in Elida,

Mary said, "Here come 18 years of total commitment."

But we knew we were in it for the long haul. The rest of our life was about to begin.

After years of searching, I was sure this was where I wanted and needed to be, grateful I had finally stumbled into happiness.

Author

M ichael Schoenhofer is the Executive Director of the Mental Health and Recovery Services Board serving the Ohio counties Allen, Auglaize, and Hardin where he plans and oversees mental health and addiction treatment and prevention programs for residents from children to seniors. Prior to that he worked in foster care, lived in Africa for six years, served in parishes in Tiffin and Toledo Ohio for 5 years where he taught high school.

Michael has a degree in psychology from St. Meinrad College, Indiana; a Master in Theology from The Gregorian University in Rome; and a Master in Social Work from the Ohio State University.

Michael writes a regular blog called Overflow at www.overflow.care. He lives in Lima Ohio with his wife, his cat Calvin, and occasionally one of his children who needs shelter.